SHARED
GOVER

THE POLITY OF

THE
EPISCOPAL
CHURCH

a collection of essays
prepared by

The House of Deputies Special Study Committee
on Church Governance and Polity

Committee Members

Canon Bonnie Anderson D.D., President, House of Deputies
The Rev. Canon Ernest L. Bennett
The Rev. Vanessa Glass, Secretary
The Rev. Tobias Stanislas Haller BSG, Chair
Sally A. Johnson Esq.
The Very Rev. Charles E. Osberger
Ms. Susannah W. Perkinson
The Hon. Byron Rushing
The Rev. Dr. James B. Simons, Vice-Chair
Mrs. Katherine Tyler Scott
The Rev. Dr. Francis H. Wade

Church Publishing
NEW YORK

© 2012 by The House of Deputies Special Study
Committee on Church Governance and Polity

A catalog record of this book is available from the Library
of Congress.

Church Publishing, Incorporated
445 Fifth Avenue
New York, New York 10016

www.churchpublishing.org

978-0-89869-872-5 (pbk.)
978-0-89869-883-1 (ebook)

5 4 3 2 1

Contents

Introduction

Bonnie Anderson, President, The House of Deputies

Shortly after the adjournment of the 76th General Convention, the President of the House of Deputies created and charged a House of Deputies Study Committee on Church Governance and Polity. The membership of the Study Committee, composed of a mix of seasoned and newer deputies, accepted the mandate to study the history, theology, political structure and practical realities of The Episcopal Church governance and polity, to explain why The Episcopal Church has historically embraced and legitimized laity, bishops and clergy equally to take their place in the governance of the Church, to identify what strengths and challenges flow from our system of governance and to make recommendations to strengthen our self-understanding based upon the findings of the Study Committee.

Why it is important now to understand our governance and polity

The way in which we govern ourselves is intrinsic to our identity as The Episcopal Church. The foundational theological principle embodied in our governance system is summarized by Saint Paul's doctrine that embraces the belief that each member of the church has a valuable gift to offer to God's work of reconciliation. The church is at its best when all members work together and embrace Saint Paul's organic doctrine in the councils of our church with equal voice and vote. This takes place in vestries, diocesan conventions, standing committees, diocesan councils, Executive Council, committees and commissions, and at General Convention. In fact, the way in which we make decisions is so much a part of our identity that it is easy to overlook the many ways in which our governance supports our faith.

Historically, in the process of reaching decisions, the House of Deputies and the House of Bishops have often expressed different opinions. Expressing differing opinions can create tensions, and there is nothing new in the tensions that may be created as the two houses grapple with important matters that are close to our hearts. Many of the deputies and bishops who have gone before us have found that differing opinions and discussion contribute to our strength. We learn from each other, and we are brought closer to God as we explore and develop our relationships honestly and with generosity of spirit.

The House of Deputies Study Committee and I offer this resource now because The Episcopal Church is at a turning point of possible change. Grounded and empowered by our history, we need to be clear about why we govern ourselves the way we do, and at the same time draw on our creative resources to discern how our governance serves and enables us to do God's reconciling work.

This is an exciting and challenging time for God's Episcopal Church. As the President of the House of Deputies, John Coburn, said of General Convention in 1973, "We have to gather ourselves together with spirit and direction." This is as true today as it was then.

To Govern and to Lead

Tobias Stanislas Haller BSG

The Episcopal Church operates under a system of shared government and leadership in which all members of the church have the capacity to play a part. Before exploring how we came to adopt this system, it might be helpful to think for a moment about the relationship between leadership and governance.

Leadership tends to be an individual quality or gift—as one says, someone "is a born leader," or another "has leadership skills." Sometimes, however, leadership responsibility comes with the office— one expects leadership from those in executive positions. But whether official or charismatic, leadership appears to work most effectively when exercised by an individual. This is true in part because of another aspect of leadership: it often involves movement or change.

Governance, on the other hand, is most often both a shared exercise, and one that involves restraint or caution. The governor on a steam engine or other mechanical device is designed to keep it from running too quickly, and the governance mechanisms of institutions are similarly designed to regulate their operation.

Governance in The Episcopal Church shows both of these qualities: it is shared by laity, clergy, and bishops, and it serves to spread the decision-making in such a way that change is usually marked by restraint until a relatively high level of consensus is achieved. Very few decisions can be taken in the church, from the parish through the General Convention, without the participation of laity and clergy—and in many cases, especially in life beyond the parish, the bishop(s). Governance in The Episcopal Church is shared.[1]

The structures of shared governance of the parish—with priest, vestry, wardens and the parish meeting all having a role in the ordered life of the congregation—find similar though not identical analogues in the diocese (bishop, standing committee, diocesan convention) and the general or international church[2] (Presiding Bishop, Executive Council, General Convention). This kind of organic structure allows for considerable resiliency, and provides many opportunities both for individuals to exercise leadership, and for larger gatherings to consult and confer as they adopt policies and programs for the good of the church.

Another important—and related—aspect of governance in The Episcopal Church is *subsidiarity*. This is the notion that decision-making should only be referred to a central governing body if and when the decision or action cannot be taken more locally. In practical terms this means that while the General Convention is the unitary authority for the governance of the whole church, in many areas it lays out broad guidelines which are implemented as local circumstances require. A good example of this is the canonical requirement (CC I.14.1) that parishes have vestries, while leaving the manner of their selection, term of office, and qualifications of voters for local implementation and action.

The concept of subsidiarity has received a good deal of attention in relation to the Anglican Communion, but it was discerned in the formative period of The Episcopal Church, in gatherings of church leaders prior to the first fully formed General Convention. For instance, at 1784 meetings in Boston and Pennsylvania, clergy and laity adopted basic "principles of ecclesiastical union" which included the following:

---

[1] In the early years of The Episcopal Church, due to the small number of bishops and concerns in some quarters about their having too much authority (charges of "prelacy" were common), bishops, while exercising a significant role in leadership, did not at the beginning have a part in the restraining role of governance. In the original Constitution of 1789, the House of Bishops (which would come into being once there were three of them) did not have the power absolutely to veto resolutions adopted by the House of Clerical and Lay Deputies. Initially in 1804, and finally in 1808 (it requiring the action of two consecutive sessions of the General Convention to amend the Constitution), the House of Bishops was granted the power to overrule any resolution of the House of Deputies, though a clause remained in effect that if the bishops did not respond within three days with either approval or rejection, acts of the House of Deputies would stand on their own authority. Although repeated efforts were made through the following century to remove this inequality, it was not until 1901 that concurrence by both Houses became absolutely required for adoption of resolutions. (WD, 13-18)

[2] I use the term "international church" here to highlight the fact that The Episcopal Church, while contiguous with the United States, also includes jurisdictions and dioceses beyond its borders.

"That no power be delegated to a general ecclesiastical government, except such as can not conveniently be exercised by the clergy and vestries, in their respective congregations." (White 1820, Appendix E) Certain powers, such as the establishment of a common liturgy and Canon Law, including modes of discipline, would naturally require central coordination—but a large part of the work of the church in its ministry and mission would take place "at the edges."

This notion of subsidiarity reflects the language Saint Paul uses when he portrays the church as a body: the body is a whole, and the parts work for the good of the whole, with each part having its distinctive gift to share or contribution to make to the common good. The work of the parts is for the good of the whole body, which is built up by their cooperation. In contemporary terms, it is a network: some organs are more vital than others, but the loss of any will alter or impair the functioning of the whole—and it is the whole body that ultimately assures the good health of the organs, coordinating their various contributions to the whole. The church, in this image, is not a mere collection of interchangeable parts, but an organic unity that lives by the cooperation of each member.

It is also important to note the degree of trust inherent in the governing structures of The Episcopal Church. This system of trust is demonstrated not only in the election of such explicit trustees as those on the boards of the Church Pension Fund and the General Theological Seminary, but in the roles played by bishops and deputies in the life of General Convention. Bishops are elected, and ordained and consecrated through mechanisms that involve the whole church (a diocese cannot simply choose and ordain its own bishop, but must obtain consent from a majority of all of the diocesan bishops and either the standing committees or the House of Deputies). Bishops are entrusted with a particular role in guarding "the faith, unity, and discipline of the Church." (BCP, 517) Deputies are elected as members of the whole church as it subsists in their own diocese, not merely as representatives of those dioceses but as persons entrusted to make decisions for the good of the whole church. A similar kind of trust is placed in parish vestries and standing committees by those who elect the members of these bodies.

A note on origins

It is common wisdom that if you want to know where you are it is helpful to retrace how you got there. This is one of the virtues and benefits of studying history.

As noted earlier, laity, clergy, and bishops all have their roles to play in the governance of the church. Obviously this is not the case in all Christian churches, nor even in all Anglican churches, at least to the same extent as it is true in TEC. Given the fact that our church proudly identifies itself as "Episcopal," one might think that the bishops had the corner on leadership and governance. But as William White's essay, "The Case of the Episcopal Churches . . . Considered," shows, the churches in the colonies (and the early states) saw themselves and identified themselves as "Episcopal" even though the only bishop involved was (as Tevye's fellow villagers said of the Czar) "far away from us" in London. (A number of appeals for a resident bishop were made over the course of the colonial period, but although this was considered by the English authorities, they took no positive action to provide a domestic episcopate.)

The physical absence of an Anglican *bishop* on North American shores did not prevent the church in the colonies from functioning *as episcopal*, but it had the practical effect of limiting the ease by which clergy could be provided to serve the needs of the church—ordination meant either coming from England originally, or (in the case of a colonial seeking orders) making the round trip to England.[3] As Bishop E. L. Parsons notes in the second chapter of *The Anglican Communion: A Survey,*

> The American daughter of the Church of England had hard going for a long time after the War of Independence. In six colonies there had been a quasi-establishment of the Church; but there was practically no organization beyond the local parish. The supervision of the Bishop of London was exercised through commissaries who were not always successful. Clergy sent out from England were often of poor quality, although the popular notion that they were all ne'er-do-wells is not true. It was difficult to

---

[3] Even after The Episcopal Church had its own resident bishops, the topic of allowing clergy from non-Episcopal traditions assisting in its work when there were few Episcopal clergy available came up on a regular basis. The small proportion of clergy to laity in the early decades of the church's life helped to shape the strong tradition of lay leadership and governance.

recruit a native ministry. The long voyage to England was necessary for ordination. Add to all this the fact that the Revolution found, as was natural, many of the clergy, English-born, loyal to the crown, and one understands why the growth of the Church was slow...Indeed, forty years after its organization was completed in 1789 it could muster only about 30,000 communicants, one out of more than four hundred of the population. (Wand, 22)

When independence came, all linkage with the Bishop of London—tenuous as it had been—was formally broken. Still, the episcopal character of the church remained unchanged. Although William White undertook consideration of an "episcopal" church without bishops—as he later himself noted, this was only because of concerns that the succession might not be obtainable if the American Revolution were entirely successful. (White 1820, Appendix E) The vexing question was how to obtain clergy—and it was to meet this need that much of the early business of the nascent church concerned the problem of how to obtain bishops—not how to do without them—and White himself not only supported the acquisition of bishops, but was himself one of the first.

The "Fundamental Principles" adopted in the 1784 New York meeting of clergy (four of whom would later become bishops) and laity from most of the states, established the rule both that "the Episcopal Church in each State, send deputies to the Convention, consisting of Clergy and Laity," and that "in every State where there shall be a bishop duly consecrated and settled, he shall be considered as a Member of the Convention, *ex Officio*." (Perry 1881, "The Preliminary Meetings")

At the same time, in spite of the fact that the laity in the colonial church exercised significant roles in both leadership and governance, there was some resistance to lay participation, particularly in New England—just as there was some opposition to the episcopate, particularly in its more prelatial form. Out of these struggles, the balance achieved in the early days of The Episcopal Church—including leadership and governance by laity, clergy, and bishops—represents a model for the church which, while not unique, is certainly distinctive of The Episcopal Church.

The ultimate question, Why?

There is behind all of these governmental structures a vital *raison d'être*—the body of the church exists for *mission*. As Archbishop William Temple famously observed, "The church is the only cooperative society in the world that exists for the benefit of those who are not its members." In a very real sense the church continues the *mission* of Christ as the incarnate and active *Body* of Christ.

Like any living body, the church is made up of members who enter and participate and then move out of participation—or as the classic view would have it, out of participation in the church militant to enter the church triumphant. Yet in spite of the change in the cast of characters, the play is still the same: the church endures as an entity in spite of the fact that the members making it up change over time. As Richard Hooker put it,

> ...The Church is always a visible society...; not an assembly, but a Society...Assemblies are properly rather things that belong to a Church...assembled for performance of public actions; which actions being ended, the assembly dissolveth itself and is no longer in being, whereas the Church which was assembled doth no less continue afterwards than before. (Hooker, III.I)

All human institutions, if they are to endure beyond a single human life-span, will be made up of individuals who contribute, from their own life experience, to the life of the whole. This division of labor (both at any given time and over time) is evident in the polity of The Episcopal Church. Bishops serve in the House of Bishops *ex officio*, from ordination through and including retirement[4]; while deputies must stand for election and serve for finite terms, though without a limit on the number of terms served. There are bishops and deputies both who may serve for decades. All members of General Convention, whether bishops, clergy or laity, bring their life experience with them to the Convention, along with the concerns of their dioceses, and join in what Hooker would call the "assembly" (of any particular session of General Convention) for the purpose of taking actions for the well-being both of the whole church and their particular circumstances. A depth of concern, and the breadth and scope of awareness both of the

---

[4] See the essay on the House of Bishops for more detail concerning the various canonical nuances on episcopal service in the House.

needs of the world and the call to mission are not restricted to any one order of ministry, and the sum of the church is ultimately greater than the mere aggregate of the thinking and work undertaken at any one session of the General Convention.

It remains a fact that there are significant numbers of new deputies as well as new bishops at any single General Convention, and the requirement that Constitutional changes be adopted in two consecutive Conventions virtually guarantees that different "assemblies" of individuals will be heard on any give change before it becomes active for the whole "society." As noted at the outset of this essay, this imparts a particularly *conservative* note to the polity of The Episcopal Church, balancing the energetic leadership of individual clergy, bishops and lay persons.

Some Thoughts on History and Theology

Frank Wade

One of the formative documents of Episcopal Church polity is William White's 1782 essay "The Case of the Episcopal Churches in the United States Considered." I believe the document is still important for developing our own understanding of our polity.

If the inclusion of priests, deacons and laity in our church councils was simply due to a lack of bishops in the country, it could be considered an act of expediency. And if it were established for expediency, it could equally be discounted if expediency called for it.

This urge to do away with the input of clergy and laity is not as far-fetched as it might seem. During the 2009 General Convention, President of the House of Deputies Bonnie Anderson invited Deputies Byron Rushing, Sally Johnson, Jim Simons and myself, along with some others, to a private conversation with Archbishop of Canterbury Rowan Williams. Our purpose was to impress upon him the importance of the House of Deputies in our polity. While assuring us that he knew all about it, he said that he had asked the House of Bishops to interpret the actions of General Convention and articulate the official position of The Episcopal Church because it was difficult to talk with us if we only meet every three years. This forms, essentially, an argument for discounting or ignoring the House of Deputies on the basis of expediency.

This makes it important for us to grasp that our polity is grounded in a firm ecclesiology and supported by history. We did not come to rely on the judgment of clergy and laity simply because we had no bishops in the beginning.

White establishes the ancient precedent that bishops were historically elected by the clergy and people. "The primitive churches were generally supplied by popular elections; even in the city of Rome, the privilege of electing the bishop continued with the people to the tenth or eleventh century; and near those times there are resolves of councils, that none should be promoted to ecclesiastical dignities, but by election of the clergy and people." (Chapter 2)

The Council of Constance (1414-1417) was convened partly to address the problem created by the election of three popes, each one claiming to have ultimate authority. The Council introduced two important elements that inform our current polity. The first is the claim of supreme authority for such a council by asserting that it "holds its power direct from Christ; everyone, no matter his rank or office, even if it be papal, is bound to obey it." The second is that the Council of Constance included the usual prelates but also laity, as representatives of "the Nations"—referring to European princes. Each Nation had six representatives. The election of a new pope required the approval of two thirds of the cardinals *and* two thirds of the representatives of each Nation.

White notes that English church decisions required the approval of Parliament, a lay body in its House of Commons. And he reminds us that Richard Hooker, to whom Anglicanism is deeply indebted, maintained that church decisions need the support of the whole community—"It is the general consent of all that giveth [church decisions] the form and vigour of laws." (Chapter 2)

In the eighteenth century The Episcopal Church was not of one mind about the source and grounding of church decisions. The issue was not just one of power but was also a conviction about how God speaks to and through God's church. Clara Loveland in *The Critical Years* maintains that division on the issue was sharp and that there was a danger of establishing two American churches on the basis of just that question. The view that bishops were sufficient for decision-making was based in Connecticut. The view that all orders including laity have a role in those decisions was found in the mid-Atlantic and South. Samuel Seabury was representative of the former; William White of the latter.

While a student at the College of Philadelphia, White was introduced to and impressed by the writings of John Locke (1632–1704). The *Stanford Encyclopedia of Philosophy* describes Locke's view of authority in this way: "Much of Locke's work is characterized by opposition to authoritarianism. This opposition is both on the level of the individual person and on the level of institutions such as government and church. For the individual, Locke wants each of us to use reason to search after truth rather than simply accept the opinion of authorities or be subject to superstition."

White's proposal for General Convention—that "The continental representative body may consist of a convenient number from each of the larger districts, formed equally of clergy and laity, and among the clergy, formed equally of presiding ministers and others; to meet statedly once in three years," (Chapter 3)—is based solidly on Locke and the interpretation of church history cited above.

Bishops are excluded from this formula because of their absence in the country at the time of White's writing. Yet White himself was convinced of the apostolic authority of bishops. "To those who, being adverse to the Apostolic origin of Episcopacy, have considered [White] as having consented with them in opinion, he is ready to declare on every suitable opportunity that the contrary was intended to be implied." (*Bishop White's Opinions,* Henry M. Onderdonk, 1846)

The current structure of The Episcopal Church reflects these convictions: the voice of the episcopate, as well as that of the lay and clerical deputies, is jointly required for the decisions and actions of the church.

The Role and Place of Laity in The Episcopal Church

Susannah W. Perkinson

The place and active role of lay people in The Episcopal Church is extensive. At the local level elected members of each worshiping community form a vestry which "shall be agents and legal representatives of the parish." (CC, I.14.2) Congregations (in some cases through their vestries, in others via the parish meeting) elect delegates to diocesan conventions; lay and ordained delegates of the diocesan conventions elect lay and ordained deputies to General Convention, and elect bishops for their dioceses. Baptized members of the faith community serve widely on committees, commissions, boards and agencies locally and at the church-wide level. TEC reflects a broad and inclusive pattern of governance which is based on the conviction that the Spirit speaks and acts through the whole community.

Our catechism answers the question, What is the ministry of the laity? as follows:

> The ministry of lay persons is to represent Christ and his Church; to bear witness to him wherever they may be; and according to the gifts given to them, to carry on Christ's work of reconciliation in the world; and **to take their place in the life, worship, and governance of the Church**. (BCP, 855)

The place of laity in governance is so essential that the first article of our Constitution affirms that General Convention cannot speak conclusively without the concurrence of lay and clerical deputies with the bishops.

In addition to firmly placing lay people in a centrally active place in the life and governance of the church, this catechetical statement echoes the promises Episcopalians make at baptism. In this commitment to a new and demanding way of life, grounded in a desire to know God and Christ for a lifetime, Episcopalians make five promises: communal prayer and fellowship, repentance and renewal, evangelism, service to others, and seeking justice and peace among all people. (BCP, 304, 305 and Thompsett 2010, 22)

Verna Dozier, a great biblical teacher and advocate for the ministry of lay members of The Episcopal Church, rightly connects these ministry responsibilities with governance roles when she writes, "Religious authority comes with baptism, and it is nurtured by prayer, worship, bible study, and life together." (Dozier, 115)

William Stringfellow, another particularly articulate and prolific Episcopal lay theologian (although he refused to define himself in those terms) called baptism "the sacrament of the laity" which confers authority on them to take their place within the polity of the church. (Stringfellow, 159)

Further, the catechetical reference to lay persons bearing witness to Christ and taking their place in the life, worship, and governance of the church "according to the gifts given them" echoes some of our earliest understandings of church organization and relationships found in Paul's writings. In 1 Corinthians 12:7, "Each is given the manifestation of the Spirit for the common good." Ephesians 4:11-12 picks up the theme by affirming that all orders of ministry have responsibility for "building up the body of Christ." Paul's focus is on attending to the *common good* and he believed that authority was dispersed throughout the community for just this purpose. All were bearers of the Spirit and all were responsible. (1 Corinthians 12:13)

Interestingly, Paul's writing to the church at Corinth occurred because of significant conflict generated by a community in which superiority was claimed by some individuals based on their possessing certain spiritual gifts. Many other problems had emerged: divisions, sects, interpersonal strife, ethical issues, moral dilemmas. Paul's response was to place emphasis on the variety of gifts which contributed to the common good rather than of any particular gift or individual. (Borg and Crossan, 200, 204)[5]

Further, Paul's communities have been referred to as "share communities" in which people took care of each other, sharing material as well as spiritual resources, in a time of significant economic fragility. (Borg and Crossan, 188) Paul emphasized everyone's equal participation and distributive justice.

The relatively flat organization of Paul's communities based in spiritual gifts and charisms rather than a hierarchical structure, could result in some degree of confusion and disorganization. (Ehrman, #3) Within a generation, by the time of 1 Clement, a different kind of church structure emerged: presbyters were given oversight. Similarly in the deutero-Pauline pastoral epistles of the New Testament (1 and 2 Timothy and Titus) there are descriptions of overseers (bishops) and deacons in charge of various aspects of church life. (Ehrman, #3) For a variety of reasons rooted in the pressures of surviving external persecution and internal doctrinal disputes, hierarchy began to appear and became more pronounced over time.[6]

The Reformation era (1500s) was marked by violence and a widening disparity between landholders and the poor. It was a time of famine, disease, and significant social instability. (Thompsett 1989, 65) The English Reformation took a particular form with the Elizabethan Settlement that shied away from adherence to a particular confession or strict doctrinal position. This matured Anglicanism was marked by broad-mindedness and a reasoned approach to biblical authority (Thompsett 1989, 66) and a comprehension of difference of opinion

---

[5]   Frank Wade has noted, "The early church's theology of the Holy Spirit was not dependent on hierarchy. Luke introduces John the Baptist by listing all of the people with titular authority (emperor, governor, rulers, high priests) then asserting that 'The Word of God came to John, son of Zechariah, in the wilderness.'"

[6]   Wade further explains some of the origins of hierarchy:

The first generation expected the end of the world in a few days and so they did not establish any system that tempered or refined the authority of the apostles. Later generations were pressed by persecution which necessitated a centralization of authority—sort of like the war time powers of a president. Such situations do not have the freedom to rely on lengthy group process.

When the persecutions ended under Constantine, the church immediately fell into controversy over the creeds. There had been no opportunity to explore the various understandings of the Gospel while the church was literally and figuratively underground. The controversies relied heavily on theological elites who added a new dimension to the developing hierarchy. The Nicene Creed was barely dry on paper when the Roman Empire collapsed, leaving the church as the only institution capable of governing on more than a local scale.

on controversial issues. Some central principals still are evident today, especially as expressed in the governance and polity of The Episcopal Church.

- We work to accommodate differing points of view.
- Church membership is based in baptism, not an adherence to a particular confession.
- There is a basic commitment that all people, lay and ordained, be educated and biblically literate.
- We have a Book of Common Prayer.

In particular, Thomas Cranmer wrote our collect for Proper 28 (BCP, 236) praying for all of us to "hear, read, mark, learn and inwardly digest" Holy Scripture. It is the Anglican way for *all* to study and discern biblical passages with a special commitment to communal deliberation and dialogue. (Thompsett 1989, 73) From Cranmer's perspective no one person or select group is the keeper of interpretation or meaning, but rather the church as a whole. This view was endorsed in the seventeenth century by the Authorized Version of the Bible which, unlike other versions, had no footnotes to tell the reader how to interpret various passages.

In the words of Bonnie Anderson, President of the House of Deputies,

> During our lifetime, God calls us in new and different ways to do God's reconciling work in the world. Some of us will continue to be called into the ministry of the laity, according to the gifts we have been given. Some of us will be called to serve as priests and deacons, according to the gifts we have been given. Some of us will be called to serve as bishops – again, according to the gifts we have been given.

In Jesus the hierarchy becomes a circle, rooted in him and open to all Christians.

The House of Deputies in the Episcopal Church

Katherine Tyler Scott

A National Platform for Lay Leadership

> I think lay people need to study the Bible and be cognizant of church history. We do not have to become scholars, but we need to be well enough educated to know that whatever form of polity our particular denomination practices is not sacrosanct, that it developed in response to certain historical events and that it is under judgment of the faith like everything else...
>
> —Verna Dozier

These wise words of Verna Dozier, one of the noted lay theologians in The Episcopal Church, help to usher us into an important conversation about the role of laity in governance and leadership, at the highest level in the General Convention's House of Deputies, where lay and clergy deputies work as equals for the good of the whole church.

I wish to begin this reflection on the House of Deputies with a focus on the role of its lay members, in large part because this level of lay participation is so important to the identity and polity of The Episcopal Church. Many church traditions do not vest such responsibility in lay members, and questions arise concerning our choice—from the very beginning—to do so: What authority do the laity have in The Episcopal Church? What are the sources of this authority? What are the roles and responsibilities of laity in the governance of the church? Why does it matter?

These are important questions that need to be addressed from time to time, because in doing so we relearn who we are, whom we serve, and what we are called to do. This brief overview is a mere introduction to some of the answers but will hopefully inspire you to read and study more about the origins and evolution of lay involvement in the governance of The Episcopal Church.

To gain a better understanding of the role and responsibilities of laity in the development and implementation of the polity of The Episcopal Church requires a knowledge of some of its early history and founding principles that helped to shape its current identity, discipline, and practice.

Brief History of Identity and Authority of Laity

The first known occurrence of the term *laity* is found in Pope St. Clement's letter to the Corinthians (40:5) addressing what he perceived to be the unjust defrocking of a pastor by those not ordained. He used this term to describe the people "set apart" by God in the New Testament through holy baptism (Burtchaell, 353-54). For a century and a half after this event the literature is silent about the existence or role of laity. The assumption was that everyone referred to as "the people of God" included laity; and until the rise of the dominance of clergy in the Middle Ages there was a relationship that recognized differences in the role, regulation and functions of clergy and laity, but made no pejorative judgments about them. The role of laity was diminished during this time, and tended to be defined by who they were not and what they were not authorized to do. In some places their responsibilities were effectively reduced to, "Pay, pray, and obey." The Reformation(s) of the fifteenth and sixteenth centuries reversed this form of subjugation and returned to the practices of the early church which allowed laity to select the clergy, care for church property, collect offerings, present the communion elements, and read scripture.

In The Episcopal Church, the role of laity has been shaped by major internal and external political, social, and religious events. The protestant aspect of our identity distinctively commits us to the Book of

Common Prayer; and to Scripture, tradition, and reason as the basis for understanding and practicing our faith. For Anglicans, Scripture is a fundamental source of authority, but without the application of reason it is perceived as dangerous. Tradition is the result of ongoing reflection by the church on our experience of God. As a consequence, we see this experience and our understanding of God as ever-deepening and changing. Juxtaposed with this adaptive process of thoughtful reflection and thought is an appreciation for order. In these practices we participate in a pursuit of truth that opens us up to the mind of God. We never can fully know what this is but knowledge of scripture, engagement in reason, and understanding tradition are responsible ways of striving toward it.

What further distinguishes The Episcopal Church is the *full participation* of the laity in worship and governance. The Episcopal Church believes in "the priesthood of all believers" and sees baptism as the entry into the community of faith—the covenant through which we live out our Christian identity and calling. We do not believe in a hierarchical or intermediary priesthood—we believe in direct access to God through grace, prayer and communal worship. We recognize that there are different charisms in the church, and that the laity have their own gifted offering to make as members of the church. We profess in our Catechism that the ministers of the church are "lay persons, bishops, priests, and deacons." (BCP, 855) Some have described the role set apart for laity as that of being full-time witnesses for Christ. (Holmes) Being full-time witnesses for Christ has meant that laity serve both the church as an institution and the church as the source of mission to the larger world. Laity are "God's action in the world." (Colliver, 9)

Origins of the American Church

The strength and influence of lay participation was particularly evident in the early years of The Episcopal Church, attested in other essays in this collection. Lay leaders were crucial in the establishment and governance of the colonial church in America and in the evolution of The Episcopal Church. One of the earliest examples is the establishment of vestries: governing bodies that exercised considerable power over congregations and their priests. They had the power to levy taxes, hire and fire clergy, and provide social services to citizens. There were no resident bishops in the colonies, and in their absence the British Crown appointed laymen, i.e., commissaries, royal governors, etc., to assume many of the duties typically ascribed to an episcopate. The authority and balance of power between churches and these officers varied regionally but generally speaking The Episcopal Church was a lay-led institution, in which clergy were in a very small minority.

The colonial churches considered themselves to be administratively autonomous from each other while still retaining a strong connection to the Church of England. As Holmes described this reality, "The Episcopal Church was universal in faith but not in governance." When the Church was detached from its English connections at the end of the Revolutionary War, the work of reconstitution included the challenge of balancing the need for national autonomy with the desire to remain loyal to the faith and to maintain the bonds of continuity between England and America.

William White, later Bishop of Pennsylvania, developed the "Pennsylvania Plan," also known as the "Federal Plan," in which he proposed the reorganization of the church in all of the states into a single ecclesiastical entity. The key concepts outlined in White's "The Case of the Episcopal Churches in the United States Considered" concerned how Anglican churches would organize into state churches which would then be nationally organized into a unitary body. White felt that the authority to govern had to be derived from elected representatives from all of the churches united by a federal constitution. (Dator, 18) His ideas are noted as the precursor to the Constitution adopted in 1789.

The process of developing a governance structure and obtaining consensus on the Constitution took many meetings of laity and clergy over a period of seven years. By 1784 most of the states agreed that a constitution was needed for the whole church, that the Book of Common Prayer needed revision, and that bishops were essential for proper episcopal oversight. James Dator, author of *Many Parts, One Body,* provides a detailed account of the significant events leading up to the formation of The Episcopal Church. Attendees at a May 1784 meeting in New Brunswick, New Jersey, discussed the possibility of unifying the church nationally and called for a national conference of laity and clergy. This conference was held in New York and attracted representatives from Massachusetts, Rhode Island, Connecticut, New York, New Jersey, Pennsylvania, Delaware, Maryland, and Virginia.

The two Conventions held in June and September of 1786 focused on completing a draft of the Constitution and obtaining the consecration of bishops. The final version of the Constitution along with the Canons, were adopted at the Convention of 1789. It was at this same Convention that the church became *The Protestant Episcopal Church in the United States of America*; and the General Convention was created, with two Houses, and established as the governing body of The Episcopal Church. The House of Deputies was referred to as the House of Clerical and Lay Deputies. Because it preceded the House of Bishops by one convention it is sometimes referred to as "the Senior House." In 1886 it was given its present name.

The General Convention: A Shared Authority of Laity, Clergy and Bishops

Article I, Section I, of the Constitution of The Episcopal Church reads: "There shall be a General Convention of this Church, consisting of the House of Bishops and the House of Deputies, in which Houses shall sit and deliberate separately; and in all deliberations, freedom of debate shall be allowed." The Canons require that there be two Joint Sessions, one on the fifth legislative day, when there is to be the election of the Presiding Bishop; and one on the seventh legislative day for the presentation of the budget.

The General Convention has the authority to establish budget and programs, amend the Constitution and Canons, and revise the Book of Common Prayer, and to undertake any action it feels to be of import to the church and its mission and ministry.

The House of Deputies consists of lay and clergy deputies elected by their respective diocesan conventions. Each deputy has one vote, and except when a vote by orders is required or called for, the lay and clergy deputies vote together. Each deputation can include up to four clergy and four lay deputies. The House of Deputies has a President, Vice-President, Secretary, and Treasurer who are elected by the House of Deputies for a three-year term that commences at the end of the Convention and continues through the subsequent Convention. The

Secretary also serves as the Secretary of General Convention after confirmation by the House of Bishops. The House of Deputies numbers over 800 and the House of Bishops has some 300 members from 110 dioceses.

The Role and Duties of a Deputy

Deputies to General Convention are fully independent. They are not elected to represent the views of their Diocese or any constituency for that matter. Ideally, they should reflect a competent knowledge of the will of the whole church, and be able to act and speak responsibly on behalf of the whole church. Deputies are to be thoroughly prepared for their legislative duties, prayerful in their discernment of issues, patient in their deliberations, and prudent in their decisions. This is especially critical given that about a third of deputies at any given General Convention are first time deputies, and that the House of Deputies meets only once every three years. The legislative process works best when there is a solid organizational structure in place; there are clear lines of communication and accountability, good relationships between the orders, and trust, all of which take time to create. The authority to act responsibly derives from a combination of these factors. Knowledge of the polity of The Episcopal Church and the capacity to work efficiently within the given structure helps in the consideration and decision-making process of legislative activity and action.

Once General Convention is adjourned, deputies are canonically responsible for reporting the actions of General Convention to their respective diocesan conventions, especially those resolutions that affect the work of the diocese. They remain deputies until the next election of deputies.

The Legislative Process
The Origin of Resolutions

Any legislation to be considered must be presented in the form of a resolution. The Committees, Commissions, Agencies and Boards (CCABs) of The Episcopal Church submit their reports which are compiled in what is known as "The Blue Book." These are designated "A"

Resolutions. "B" Resolutions originate from bishops; "C" Resolutions come from provinces and dioceses; and "D" Resolutions are submitted by deputies. Deputies are limited to submitting three (3) resolutions and each resolution must be endorsed by at least three deputies. Those submitting resolutions are encouraged to do so at least ninety days prior to General Convention, so that they can be referred to the proper Legislative Committee at least 60 days prior to the opening of Convention. Resolutions requiring action by both Houses can be submitted during the session of Convention up until the end of the second legislative day (or later by a two-thirds vote of the members present). (HOD Rule 24)

Legislative Committees

There are 24-26 Legislative Committees in each House of the General Convention, and the President of the House of Deputies (PHOD) and President of the House of Bishops, the Presiding Bishop (PB), appoint the officers and members of these committees for each House respectively. All deputies are e-mailed a form requesting their preferences for committee membership and these are considered in the formation of the committees. The PHOD's Council of Advice may offer counsel on the selection of leadership and membership, with the final authority and decision that of the President.

Once a resolution has been submitted, one House is designated the House of Initial Action (HIA) by agreement of the Presiding Officers, and each resolution is assigned to a Legislative Committee by the Presiding Officer of each House. Those Committees in both the HOD and HOB with identical names are "cognate committees."

The legislative committees must consider every assigned resolution and hold public hearings whose venue is posted a minimum of four hours in advance. Bishops, deputies, alternates, and visitors may sign up to address the committee at the hearing. Each committee may discuss the resolution with its cognate committee and develop a recommendation for the HIA to consider. The resolution must be reviewed by the Legislative Committee on the Constitution if it proposes an amendment to the Constitution, or the Legislative Committee on Canons if proposing an amendment to the Canons. If it has funding implications it must also be reviewed by the Program, Budget and Finance (PB&F) Committee.

After hearings and discussion, the Legislative Committee from the HIA can recommend to the House that a resolution be:

1. Adopted;
2. Adopted, but with amended or substituted text;
3. Rejected;
4. Referred to a Committee, Commission, Agency or Board; or
5. that the committee be discharged from further consideration of the resolution.

Action in the House

The resolution, with the committee's recommendation, is next placed on the Daily Calendar for floor debate and vote; or on the Consent Calendar, which is placed before the House for action without debate.[7] The HIA may accept the committee's recommendation or provide its own. If the House rejects the resolution or discharges the committee from further consideration of it, it dies. If adopted, the resolution is sent to the second House's legislative committee, and follows the same process. If the Second House amends the resolution, it is sent back to the first House. Either House may originate and propose legislation, and all acts of the Convention shall be adopted and be authenticated by both Houses. A resolution becomes an Act of Convention only after both Houses adopt it in identical language.

The order of business is specified in the Rules of Order, and there is provision for a House to suspend the order or set a Special Order of Business to consider a particular question. When a committee reports on a message from the other House, it cannot postpone or table the matter. Amendments may be made, which will require return to the other House.

---

[7] In the House of Deputies a resolution may be removed from the Consent Calendar by action of "any three Lay or Clerical deputations, or (2) the sponsor of the matter, or (3) the Committee on Dispatch of Business…" (HOD Rules 6) A similar mechanism is available in the House of Bishops.

On the Floor of the House of Deputies

To expedite discussion and debate on resolutions, microphones are strategically placed throughout the House of Deputies' meeting space; for some debates specific microphones will be designated as positions from which to support or oppose a resolution. Those wishing to speak for or against the resolution line up at the microphone of their choice. Once deputies reach the microphone they wait to be recognized by the Presiding Officer before speaking, and when recognized first state their name and diocese. The amount of time for debate and frequency of speaking is determined by the Rules of Order of the House. Amendments or substitutes being proposed from the floor must be submitted in writing to the Secretary. A special order of business with special debate rules may be set for certain matters deemed important. The House of Deputies can also move into being a Committee of the Whole.

A vote by orders on any matter can be requested by the clergy or lay deputations from three (3) separate dioceses. Some actions of Convention, such as amendments to the Constitution, require a vote by orders. In a vote by orders each diocese has one vote in the clerical order and one in the lay order. An affirmative vote in each order with the deputation is decided by a majority of deputies in each order. If the vote in an order is equally divided (2-2) it has the effect of being a negative vote, since a positive majority of dioceses (in each order) is required for adoption. The vote by orders is thus a mechanism normally requiring a higher degree of consensus in order for adoption to succeed.

Each deputy is expected to be present at all sessions to exercise this vote. There is no provision for abstention. When a deputy is absent from one or more sessions, provision for an alternate deputy to be certified is provided. Voting is variously done through voice vote, standing for the ayes or nays, show of red or green cards, electronic keypads, or printed ballots.

Summary

The Outline of the Faith in the Book of Common Prayer offers these words concerning the work and role of laity:

> *The ministry of lay persons is to represent Christ and his Church; to bear witness to him wherever they may be; and, according to the gifts given them, carry on Christ's work of reconciliation in the world; and to take their place in the life, worship, and governance of the Church.*
> (BCP, 855)

The role and authority of laity "in the...governance of the Church" is unequivocally documented, voting in the House of Deputies as equal with the clergy. The polity of The Episcopal Church is characterized by this inclusion of laity, clergy and bishops as equally valued voices in policy and practice. Any erosion of the role and authority of the House of Deputies would fundamentally change the identity and character of the church.

The Work of the House of Bishops

Sally Johnson

Summary: This chapter discusses the House of Bishops as a body, not the duties and responsibilities of individual bishops or the bishops of a province acting as a body. There are three distinct ways in which the House of Bishops meets: as one House of the two-House body that is General Convention, as a House of Bishops unrelated to its role at General Convention, and as a Council of Bishops.

The House of Bishops as one House of General Convention functions under the same parameters, for the most part, as does the House of Deputies. It is a large gathering, ranging from 125 to 175 in attendance. It follows fairly strict procedures for the submission and consideration of a large volume of legislation and other actions such as elections.

Historically it met once a year for a short session in years between sessions of General Convention in order to do necessary business such as electing certain bishops and consenting to the election of others. It often issued a Pastoral Letter to the church focused on world events, particularly the plight of the poor, hungry and disadvantaged and on aspects of church life such as marriage after divorce or the ordination of women. In recent years it has spent considerable time on The Episcopal Church's relationship with the Anglican Communion in the wake of unprecedented steps by the "Instruments of Communion"[8] to deter the church from ordaining gay and lesbian candidates to the episcopate and blessing same-sex unions.

---

[8] The Archbishop of Canterbury, the Lambeth Conference, the Anglican Consultative Council, and the Primates' Meeting.

Since 1991 the Presiding Bishop has added an additional one-week meeting to the cycle of meetings, intended mostly as a retreat.

In recent years, meetings of the House of Bishops have provided its members with education on a variety of topics from media skills to handling misconduct cases, theological reflections, time for community building and fellowship, and study of issues in the Anglican Communion and the world. The business meetings are typically very short, sometimes taking a day and sometimes just a few minutes.

Brief History of the House of Bishops

As has been discussed in other chapters, it took some time to settle the role that bishops would play in what was to become The Episcopal Church. The Church of England in the colonies functioned without bishops, with few clergy, and with lay people generally in charge of the day-to-day work of the church. The lay and clergy leaders at the first meetings to form The Episcopal Church decided that there would be bishops in the church, but in the first Constitution (August 1789) the House of Bishops was created to be a "house of revision," that is, it could refuse to concur in legislation originated by the House of Deputies. However, a veto by the House of Bishops could be overruled by a three-fifths vote of the House of Deputies. In October 1789 General Convention met again, and to accommodate requests from New Englanders who had not yet joined the church and wanted a greater role for bishops, amended the Constitution to provide that the House of Bishops could also propose and originate legislation. The House of Deputies' veto over the House of Bishops' non-concurrence to legislation passed by the House of Deputies was raised from three-fifths to four-fifths.

In 1808, the Constitution was amended to remove the ability of the House of Deputies to overrule a non-concurrence by the House of Bishops. However, it also added a provision that if the House of Bishops failed to report on legislation sent to it by the House of Deputies within three days, the legislation would become an act of Convention. The "three days clause" was not deleted until 1901. (WD, 14-15)

The current Constitution first mentions the House of Bishops in Article I, Sec.1:

> There shall be a General Convention of this Church, consisting of the House of Bishops and the House of Deputies, which Houses shall sit and deliberate separately; and in all deliberations freedom of debate shall be allowed. Either House may originate and propose legislation, and all acts of the Convention shall be adopted and be authenticated by both Houses.

Membership and Voting Rights in the House of Bishops

Every organized body has to decide who can participate in it, who qualifies for membership, and the rights of each member. Just as General Convention defines membership in the House of Deputies, so has it always defined membership in the House of Bishops. In the beginning the Constitution stated merely that "The Bishops of this Church" made up the House of Bishops. "Consequently, from 1789 to 1901 the House included diocesan bishops and, at various times, assistant bishops,[9] missionary bishops, and foreign missionary bishops." (WD, 18) Despite numerous attempts, often coupled with other proposed changes on which bishops should have voting rights, suffragan bishops were not given the right to vote until 1943.

Article I, Sec. 2 of the current Constitution sets forth the bishops who have a seat and vote in the House of Bishops. Six categories of bishops are entitled to seat and vote in the House of Bishops:

- Bishops with jurisdiction (Diocesan)[10]
- Coadjutor Bishops
- Suffragan Bishops
- Assistant Bishops
- Bishops who resigned for reasons of
  - » Advanced age
  - » Bodily infirmity
  - » Election to an office created by the General Convention

---

9 Prior to 1895 assistant bishops were the equivalent of what are now Bishops Coadjutor.

10 Canon I.11.2.c provides that the Bishop of an Area Mission which is a Missionary Jurisdiction, exercises jurisdiction if he or she is a Bishop of The Episcopal Church.

» Mission strategy determined by the General Convention or the House of Bishops

In 2003, the House of Bishops adopted Standing Order X in the House of Bishops Rules of Order defining the terms in Article I.2 specifying which resigned bishops are entitled to retain their seat and vote in the House:

X. Whenever the House shall make a determination under Article I.2 of the Constitution that a resigned Bishop shall or shall not retain a seat and vote in the House, the following understanding of the intent of the pertinent terms of that provision of the Constitution shall apply:

(a) "advanced age" shall mean at least 62 years of age;

(b) "bodily infirmity" shall mean either a condition for which one is eligible for disability retirement benefits from the Church Pension Fund or Social Security Administration, or a physical or mental impairment that a physician or psychiatrist (approved by the Presiding Bishop) certifies would likely result in eligibility for such disability retirement benefits should the Bishop continue in active episcopal ministry;

(c) "office created by the General Convention" shall mean a ministry funded by the General Convention Budget and approved by the Presiding Bishop;[11] and

(d) "mission strategy" shall mean a strategy that would allow the election of an indigenous member of the clergy of a non-domestic diocese as Bishop, or that would allow a diocese to implement a new mission strategy as determined by the Presiding Bishop, or that would allow a transition in episcopal leadership after a Diocesan Bishop or Bishop Suffragan has served 10 or more years in either or both of those offices.

Depending on the circumstances of a bishop's retirement (resignation) he/she may or may not continue to have a vote in the House

---

[11] The definition of "office created by the General Convention" adopted by the House of Bishops significantly narrows the scope of the language of the Constitution, requiring an office to be "funded by the General Convention Budget and approved by the Presiding Bishop." It is not clear whether the Standing Order was intended to limit or clarify the language of the Constitution.

of Bishops. The issue of retired bishops having the right to vote has been the subject of numerous actively debated resolutions to amend the Constitution since at least 1946. (WD, 21-22)

There are bishops who are *not* entitled to seat and vote in the House of Bishops, including bishops who, when they resigned their jurisdiction or position, were under the age of 62, who were healthy (no bodily infirmity), who were not elected to an office created by General Convention and did not resign for purposes of "mission strategy." Currently (2011), there are at least seven bishops not entitled to seat and vote in the House of Bishops. Five or more are bishops who resigned their jurisdiction or position when they were less than 62 years old and not for one of the other reasons stated in Article I.2 that would allow them to keep their vote. One is the Bishop of the Convocation of American Churches in Europe.[12]

Resigned bishops who were not eligible to retain their seat and vote in the House at the time of their resignation can regain their seat and vote upon becoming an Assistant Bishop.[13] Other than becoming an Assistant Bishop, the Constitution does not explicitly provide for any other resigned bishops who did not qualify to keep their seat and vote at the time they resigned to regain that seat at some later date. The drafters of the Constitution likely assumed that a bishop with jurisdiction or a suffragan bishop who resigned other than for purposes of "mission strategy" or "upon election to an office created by General Convention" would not later be elected to be a bishop with jurisdiction or a suffragan in another diocese and so made no mention of how such a bishop would regain a vote. Despite the clear wording of Article I, Sec. 2 that whether or not a resigned bishop is entitled to seat and vote in the House of Bishops is determined at the time of their resignation, the House of Bishops has restored seat and vote to bishops who were not eligible to retain them upon their resignation but who later took a position in the church without jurisdiction.

---

[12] The Convocation functions under the terms of Canon I.15, which remain relatively flexible to provide for different circumstances. Originally served by resigned or retired Bishops, it has since 2001 elected its own bishop.

[13] An "Assistant Bishop" is defined in Canon III.12.5.a and election to the office requires a vote of the diocesan Convention desiring the services of an Assistant Bishop. Assistant Bishops should not be confused with the current practice of a Diocesan Bishop choosing to hire an "Assisting Bishop" without action by the diocesan Convention, a practice not provided for in the Constitution or Canons. Assisting Bishops may be semi- or fully retired, or have otherwise resigned from the position to which they were elected.

There are currently no provisions in the Constitution or Canons defining whether there can be members of the House without a seat or a vote. Nonetheless, in 1997 the House made provision for members with seat and voice but no vote in its Rules of Order XXV:

> Any Bishop of this Church who resigns a position for reasons other than those specified in Article 1.2 of the Constitution, but whose resignation is not for reasons related to the Bishop's moral character, may, on motion and by a majority vote, be accorded non-voting membership in the House. Until further contrary action by the House, any such non-voting member shall have the right to seat and voice at all meetings, the right to serve on committees, and all other rights of membership except that of voting on any matter.

The House also provides for the admission of "collegial" members, with seat and voice but no vote, in Rules of Order XXIV. This applies to bishops of the Anglican Communion in exile, in extra-provincial status, or who reside in any jurisdiction of The Episcopal Church. Rule XXVI also provides for "the courtesy of seat and voice" to a bishop of the Anglican Communion whose diocese is in a companion diocese relationship with a diocese of TEC or to bishops who are guests of the Presiding Bishop.[14]

Quorums and number of votes required

In every organized voting body, the minimum number of members required to be present in order to transact business, generally referred to as a "quorum" requirement, must be set. Different types of members may be treated differently; for instance, some may be entitled to vote but are not counted for purposes of determining a quorum when they are not present. Other members may be entitled to vote on

---

[14] In recent years "Provisional" bishops have been used in Southwestern Virginia, San Joaquin, Fort Worth, Pittsburgh and Quincy. The term "provisional" does not appear in the Constitution or Canons. However, Canon III.13.1 does provide that a diocese without a bishop may, by an act of its Convention, be "placed under the provisional charge and authority of a Bishop of another Diocese or of a resigned Bishop, who shall by that act be authorized to exercise all the duties and offices of the Bishop of the Diocese until a Bishop is elected and ordained for that Diocese or until the act of the Convention is revoked." Fort Worth was placed under the provisional charge of the Bishop of Kentucky, the Right Reverend Theodore Gullick while he was still the Bishop of Kentucky. While "neighboring diocese" is not defined in the Constitution or Canons, Kentucky is not contiguous with the Diocese of Fort Worth; it is in the third ring of dioceses out from Fort Worth and is in Province IV whereas Fort Worth is in Province VII. The Right Reverend Wallis Ohl, resigned bishop of Northwest Texas, succeeded Bishop Gullick in Fort Worth. That diocese is contiguous with Fort Worth but Bishop Ohl had resigned as bishop of Northwest Texas some time prior to taking charge of Fort Worth.

some matters but not on others. When a vote is being taken it must be clear not only which members have the right to vote but which members will be counted for purposes of determining whether there is a quorum, and which members will be counted to determine whether the percentage of votes needed to pass a measure has been obtained.

Art. I.2 as adopted in 1961 set the current quorum requirement:

> A majority of all Bishops entitled to vote, exclusive of Bishops who have resigned their jurisdiction or positions, shall be necessary to constitute a quorum for the transaction of business.

Prior to 1961 the quorum requirement was:

> A majority of all Bishops entitled to vote, exclusive of the Foreign Missionary Bishops, shall be necessary to constitute a quorum for the discussion of business.

In many decision-making bodies some decisions are deemed so important that more than a simple majority of those present (assuming there is a quorum) is required. Otherwise, if a quorum is a simple majority and a simple majority of those present can take action a decision could be made by only about twenty-five percent of those eligible to vote. So, as with a vote by orders in the House of Deputies or with other decisions in the House of Deputies that require a super-majority to pass, the House of Bishops takes some actions by a number greater than a simple majority of those present. Other than a two-thirds vote to suspend or override procedural Rules of Order, a matter must be passed by greater than a simple majority in the following situations:

- Article I.3 requires the election of a Presiding Bishop to be "...by a vote of a majority of all Bishops, excluding retired Bishops not present, except that whenever two-thirds of the House of Bishops are present a majority vote shall suffice..."

- Article VI.2 requires the cession or retrocession of territory of a diocese when "...such action of the General Convention,..., shall be by a vote of two-thirds of all the Bishops present and voting..."

- House of Bishops Rules of Order, General Rules for Meetings of This House XXIV requires the vote on

granting collegial membership to bishops from other
provinces of the Anglican Communion to be "by a two-
thirds vote of those present and voting on each Bishop,
taken by secret ballot if requested by at least six members
of the House..."

Another issue concerns which members are counted to determine
the number on which the majority or super-majority is calculated. In
addition to the three sections cited immediately above, two additional
provisions specify which bishops are counted for that purpose:

- Article X—voting on changes to BCP—is "by a majority
  of all Bishops, excluding retired Bishops not present,
  of the whole number of Bishops entitled to vote in the
  House of Bishops, ..."

- Canon IV.16.A.2 on the Abandonment of Communion
  by a Bishop says that the vote to consent to the bishop's
  deposition must be "by a majority of the whole number
  of Bishops entitled to vote..."

You will notice that the language in these four provisions is very similar but not identical. Recently, in the vote by the House of Bishops to
consent to the finding of Abandonment of Communion by the Bishop
of Pittsburgh the issue was raised whether the majority was based on
all the bishops entitled to vote whether or not they were present at the
meeting or only on those bishops entitled to vote actually present at
the meeting.

The method of voting, how the vote is taken, is also important. The
basic rule of voting in bodies under Robert's Rules of Order, adopted
by the House of Bishops, is that a voice vote is sufficient unless another
method is specified. If the voice vote isn't clear, the Chair may call for a
show of hands or ask members to stand. In the House of Bishops some
matters must be voted on by ballot and several by secret ballot.

Votes that must be taken by ballot include giving consent to the consecration of a bishop when requested by six bishops (House of Bishops
Rules of Order, General Rules for Meetings of This House VIII), and
the election of a Missionary Bishop (House of Bishops Rules of Order,
Missionary Bishops II). Votes that must be taken by secret ballot are
the election of the Presiding Bishop (Canon I.2.2), and the admission

of collegial members to the House of Bishops (House of Bishops Rules of Order, General Rules for Meetings of This House Rule XXIV).

In recent years significant time, energy and resources have been spent to determine exactly how the membership and voting requirements should be interpreted and applied given the differences in language between similar provisions. Uncertainty could be removed if these various provisions were clarified and, where appropriate, identical language used.

Authority and Role of the House of Bishops

According to the Constitution and Canons there are three distinct ways in which the House of Bishops functions: as one House of the two-House body that is General Convention, as a House of Bishops unrelated to its role at General Convention, and as a Council of Bishops.

House of Bishops at General Convention

One of the principal responsibilities of the House of Bishops is to participate as one of the two Houses of The Episcopal Church's General Convention. Other than the few actions each House is authorized to take without concurrent action by the other House, both Houses must concur for an action to be an act of the General Convention and hence binding on The Episcopal Church. The House of Bishops has its own Rules of Order as does the House of Deputies. Just as most of the House of Deputies Rules of Order deal with how it functions during its meeting at General Convention, so do the House of Bishops Rules of Order specify how it will deal with legislation at General Convention. In addition to their own Rules of Order, both Houses are also subject to the Joint Rules of Order. In many respects the House of Bishops functions parallel to the House of Deputies and all those procedures will not be discussed here. Its Rules of Order specify its legislative committees.

While it has become common for the cognate legislative committees of the two Houses to meet jointly to discuss and consider legislation, the committees of each House vote and report separately. There is no requirement that legislative committees of the two Houses meet together, but such a practice was in place on the part of some committees as early as 1988, in order to work out specific issues.[15] By 1994 this was becoming more common, and such a practice was strongly encouraged by the planning committee for the 1997 General Convention. The 2000 Legislative Handbook for Bishops and Deputies noted:

> Cognate Legislative Committees generally meet together, hold joint hearings on resolutions, and discuss recommendations on each of the resolutions referred to them. The practical effect of these joint meetings is that if a resolution passes the House of initial action unchanged from the Cognate Committee's recommendation, the other House is ready to place this matter on the calendar.

Sessions of the House of Bishops are similar to those of the House of Deputies in most ways. However, it is a smaller assembly, as from 125–175 of its over 250 members are usually present, compared to 800 in the House of Deputies. This scale has allowed it to function differently in some respects. There is no limit on how long a bishop may speak to an issue compared to the three minutes allowed each deputy and there is no limit on the length of debate on any issue compared to the 30-minute limitation in the House of Deputies.

In addition to considering legislation proposed by either House after consideration by the legislative committees, the House of Bishops also elects some of its members to serve on various boards and agencies, to fill various offices or functions; elects persons, whether lay, clergy or bishops to other boards, generally with the concurrence of the House of Deputies; nominates persons to fill certain offices of the Convention such as the Registrar, Recorder and Custodian of the Book of Common Prayer; and concurs with some elections by the House of Deputies.

House of Bishops between General Conventions

This section discusses the authority of the House of Bishops at meetings between General Conventions. The only explicit reference to such a meeting is in the Canon on the Presiding Bishop (I.2.4.a.4), empowering the Presiding Bishop to call a meeting of the House. The first record of such a meeting between General Convention sessions is in 1866. Between then and 1969, meetings between sessions generally took

---

15 HD Rule 51 and HB General Rule XXII provide for conferencing with the cognate committee chairs in the other House.

place at least once if not twice in the three-year period, and an annual meeting was required by Standing Order XII of the Rules of Order of the House from 1928 to 1940. The practice was maintained even with the Rule's removal. Since 1992 the House has varied the regularity of meetings, but always on a greater than annual basis.[16]

The authority of the House of Bishops between General Conventions granted in the Constitution and Canons can be generally divided into several broad categories:

- Consent to bishops' resignations
- Elect bishops for
  - » non-diocesan ministries, including the Presiding Bishop, and for dioceses upon request of the diocese
  - » Missionary Dioceses when requested by its Convention
  - » Dioceses when requested by its Convention
- Determine membership in the House of Bishops in some instances
- Authorize some disciplinary actions against bishops
- Authorize the formation process for new bishops
- Provide for continuing education of bishops
- Establish Missions within the boundaries of The Episcopal Church but outside diocesan boundaries
- Call special meetings of General Convention
- Recognize Religious Orders and Christian Communities through its Committee on Religious Communities
- Issue Pastoral Letters to the church
- Issue Position Papers to the church
- Direct the Standing Commission on Liturgy and Music to prepare for General Convention recommendations concerning the Lectionary, Psalter, and offices for special occasions

The House of Bishops in its Rules of Order and in one instance by canon has established a variety of committees. A Committee on

---

[16] Research Report: House of Bishops Interim Meetings, Archives of the Episcopal Church, June 14, 2011.

Religious Communities, a Standing Committee on the Bishops' Pastoral responsible for drafting Pastoral Letters from the House of Bishops to the church, a Standing Committee on the Resignation of Bishops and a committee to prepare Memorial Messages to the family of deceased bishops. Its Rules of Order also provides for the Advisory Committee to the Presiding Bishop commonly known as the Presiding Bishop's Council of Advice.

In addition to the committees specified by canon or its Rules of Order, the House of Bishops currently also has a Committee on Theology, Committee on Pastoral Development, Committee on Planning, and Bishops Spouses' Planning Group. Whether these committees, rules and practices adequately serve the needs of the House of Bishops is primarily a matter for that House. Whether these structures advance the mission of the church is a question for the church.

The House of Bishops often does its business, formal and informal, in private without any press or other members of the church present. The motion to enter such an executive session is provided for under General Rule XII. There are circumstances in which such privacy and confidentiality are critical, in part specified by House of Bishops Rules governing elections and appointments. However, the extent to which the House of Bishops acts in private compared to most other structures of governance in the church, is a cause for concern to a number of people. There has been controversy in recent years about the reluctance of the House of Bishops publically to identify members of various committees or task groups. As a result, in 2009 General Convention passed a resolution requiring that the membership of all committees and other such bodies, elected or appointed by virtually all governance structures of the General Convention, be publically available within thirty days after election or appointment.

Council of Bishops

Canon I.2.4.a.4, on the duties and responsibilities of the Presiding Bishop, provides:

> The Presiding Bishop...shall:
>
> > (4) Take order for the consecration of Bishops, when duly elected; and, from time to time, assemble the Bishops of

the Church to meet, either as the House of Bishops or as
a Council of Bishops, and set the time and place of such
meetings;

This is the only reference to the House of Bishops as a "Council of Bishops" in the current (2009) Constitution, Canons and Rules of Order.

From a review of Journals of the General Convention it does not appear that the House has been called to meet in this way very often, or in recent history.

Mind of the House Resolutions

Although not provided for or referenced anywhere in the Constitution or Canons or the House of Bishops Rules of Order, some time in the past fifty years or so the House of Bishops began adopting "Mind of the House" resolutions on various topics. Among these was the 1977 "Port St. Lucie conscience clause" adopted a year after the General Convention approved the ordination of women. Port St. Lucie was the location of the House of Bishops' meeting at which the resolution was adopted. It stated, in part:

> (4) In the light of all this and in keeping with our intention
> at Minneapolis, we affirm that no Bishop, Priest, Deacon
> or Lay Person should be coerced or penalized in any
> manner, nor suffer any canonical disabilities as a result
> of his or her conscientious objection to or support of
> the 65th General Convention's action with regard to the
> ordination of women to the priesthood or episcopate.

Over time, the church tended to forget that this was a resolution of the House of Bishops alone, rather than a resolution of the General Convention, far less a canonical requirement. Over time, many in the church assumed the "Conscience Clause" *was* part of the canon on the ordination of women or that it had been a condition on which the passage of women's ordination was premised. It was adopted by the House of Bishops alone a year *after* the General Convention authorized the ordination of women to the priesthood and episcopate.

More recently, after the consecration of Bishop Gene Robinson, and in response to the Windsor Report's request for a moratorium on the consecration of gay and lesbian bishops, the House of Bishops adopted a Mind of the House Resolution committing the members of the House of Bishops not to consent to the consecration of *any* bishop from the time of the resolution's adoption until at least the 2006 General Convention. The subsequent 2006 General Convention rejected such a moratorium but adopted Resolution B033 strongly encouraging bishops and Standing Committees to refrain from consenting to the consecration of any bishop-elect whose "manner of life" would put further strains on the Anglican Communion. This resolution deliberately avoided specifying partnered gay and lesbian clergy. In response to strong negative reactions by leaders in the wider Anglican Communion to the resolution, at its next meeting the House of Bishops adopted a Mind of the House Resolution purporting to interpret Resolution B033 stating that gays and lesbians *were* intended to be included as persons whose "manner of life" would cause further strains on communion.

While the House of Bishops is certainly free to express its opinions, it is not allowed to contradict or interpret the canons or resolutions of General Convention. Mind of the House Resolutions are not part of the "Discipline of the Church" (CC IV.2). They are not binding on the church, as only the concurrent action of the House of Bishops and House of Deputies at the General Convention can bind the church. In *Stanton v. Righter*, the Court for the Trial of a Bishop considered the binding nature of House of Bishops resolutions:

> The first four of these documents are statements or resolutions by the House of Bishops or by the Presiding Bishop and his Council of Advice. They do not express the decision of the Church acting it its corporate capacity through General Convention. They alone cannot establish the doctrine of The Episcopal Church nor command the Church's obedience and discipline. (Opinion of the Court, May 15, 1996, 15-16)

Ultimately, a Mind of the House Resolution expresses the opinion of those bishops present at a particular meeting of the House of Bishops who voted for the resolution, and it cannot even bind those who voted for it.

The House of Bishops does have authority to issue Pastoral Letters and Position Papers. While the canonical authority of the House of Bishops is focused primarily on the status of bishops in the church and providing Missionary Areas with a bishop to build the church, much of their time together is spent looking at the state of the world—natural disasters, poverty, injustice, war, nuclear threats, civil unrest, and racism, and in formulating Pastoral Letters or their equivalent about these issues addressed to the church and often to Congress or other groups or bodies. These Pastoral Letters express the view of the House of Bishops on these issues. Another focus of their time and Pastoral Letters has been the state of the church, the need for its people to live holier lives and to focus their lives on prayer, action, evangelism and stewardship. The House of Bishops provides strong leadership to the church through its Pastoral Letters and statements about the state of the world and the urgency for the church and its members to be actively involved in responding to physical and spiritual needs of our broken world.[17]

The Constitution and Canons on the Authority of the House of Bishops

The Canons specifying that the House of Bishops elects persons to various bodies and positions or has to consent to elections by the House of Deputies are *not* set forth below. These duties are important in the overall governance of the church, and their omission here does not indicate any intent to diminish that importance. References to the authority for a majority or other specified number of bishops to take an action even if it does not have to be taken in the context of a meeting of the House of Bishops are set forth below.

Constitution

- Article II
  - » Section 6. The House of Bishops must give its consent to a bishop's resignation of jurisdiction.
  - » Section 7. The House of Bishops elects a Suffragan Bishop for the chaplains in the Armed Forces, Veterans'

---

[17] Its position statements addressed to Congress and other entities or leaders outside the church are a powerful witness as well. Some of these statements enter into areas of responsibility of both the General Convention and Executive Council, bodies with the authority to set the policies and positions for the church—and in which the bishops have roles as a House at General Convention and as individuals chosen as members of Executive Council. House of Bishops' statements in this area may be duplicative of positions taken on behalf of the church by General Convention or Executive Council and may result in confusion as to who speaks for The Episcopal Church and what the official position of the church is on any particular issue.

Administration Medical Centers, and Federal Correctional Institutions.

» Section 8. The House of Bishops must consent to the resignation and renunciation of the right of succession of a Bishop Coadjutor elected as a bishop in another diocese.

- Article III: The House of Bishops must consent to the consecration of Bishops for foreign lands.

- Article VI

» Section 1. The House of Bishops may establish Missions in any area not within the boundaries of this Church and elect or appoint a bishop for such Mission.

Canons

- Title I—Organization and Administration

» Canon I.1.3.a—A majority of bishops can requisition or must consent to the calling of a special meeting of General Convention;

» Canon I.1.5.c—The House of Bishops prescribes the forms of Letters of Ordination and Consecration.

» Canon I.2.1.e—The House of Bishops elects the Presiding Bishop with the consent of the House of Deputies.

» Canon I.2.1.f—The House of Bishops elects a person to fill a vacancy in the office of Presiding Bishop with the consent of a majority of Standing Committees.

» Canon I.11.2.a—The House of Bishops may establish a Mission in any area not within the boundaries of a diocese of this church, or of a church in communion with this church and the House of Bishops approves the conditions and agreements related to the Mission.

- Title III—Ministry

» Canon III.11.1.b—The House of Bishops elects a bishop for a diocese upon request of the Convention of the diocese. The House of Deputies or a majority of Standing Committees must approve the election.

» Canon III.11.10.c—The House of Bishops elects a bishop for a Missionary Diocese upon request of the Convention of the Missionary Diocese. The election must be approved by a majority of Standing Committees.

» Canon III.12.8.d—The House of Bishops accepts or refuses the resignation of bishops.

» Canon III.14.1—The Committee on Religious Communities of the House of Bishops must officially recognize Religious Orders and Christian Communities.

» Canon III.15.1—The House of Bishops fills any vacancies on the General Board of Examining Chaplains between General Conventions.

- Title IV—Ecclesiastical Discipline

  » Canon IV.17.7.a—The House of Bishops may issue a Statement of Disassociation from doctrine alleged to be contrary to that held by this Church upon filing of a request for it.

  » Canon IV.17.7.b—One-third of the House of Bishops must approve of a request to initiate proceedings against a bishop for an Offense of Doctrine.

  » Canon IV.18.A—The House of Bishops must consent to the deposition of a bishop for Abandonment of the Communion.

The Provincial Structure
of The Episcopal Church

Jim Simons

The concept of a provincial system (dividing the church into geographic regions) is older than The Episcopal Church itself and arguably has engendered more controversy than any other polity concept in our history. The purpose and functionality of the provinces have long been debated and there is currently little agreement as to their ultimate value.

The earliest notion of dividing The Episcopal Church into districts or provinces was suggested by William White in 1782. White, still the rector of Christ Church Philadelphia, wrote a treatise on the organization of the nascent church. While "The Case of The Episcopal Churches" is probably most noteworthy for White's pragmatic treatment of the episcopacy (he thought we could do without it for a while if necessary), he also suggested the idea of dividing the entire body into three geographical districts.

These districts would hold annual conventions with deputies from every congregation or group of congregations which could support a rector, and these conventions would order the common life of the church within the district. White also suggested that what would become known as the General Convention would meet every three years and that deputies (lay, ordained, bishops) representing each of the three districts would constitute General Convention. (White 1782, 25-26)

White suggested such a system because the vast distances deputies were required to travel for a General Convention would make frequent national gatherings difficult. Smaller districts would provide easier access for congregations to be represented. Although not explicitly stated, White certainly implies the principle of subsidiarity, that the districts would be accountable to the "Continental Convention" and refer continental concerns to that level. It would also seem that White did not anticipate conventions at the "State" (diocesan) level.

White's proposal was very much in outline form. When the first General Conventions began to develop a structure for our polity the concept of such provinces or districts was not put in place.

At the General Convention of 1850, two separate but related resolutions were proposed by the House of Bishops regarding provinces. The precipitating reason was the need for a convenient court of appeals in matters of clergy discipline. Bishop Hopkins of Vermont proposed that the entire church be divided into an unspecified number of "districts" each containing between three and eight bishops. These bishops would be responsible for hearing appeals in disciplinary cases within their district. (JGC 1850, 145)

Bishop DeLancey of Western New York had a rather more ambitious idea that the church be divided into four districts, each of which would be responsible for ordering its common life in all aspects except "Prayer Books, Articles, Offices, and Homilies of this Church" which would fall under the purview of the General Convention, which would meet every twenty years. (JGC 1853, 146)

While the convention of 1856 considered this, what was ultimately proposed was an appellate system which involved the entire House of Bishops. This did not pass and neither did another proposal dividing the church into four geographical districts. Taylor (148) has suggested that the suspicion with which these plans were regarded was based on the principle of "state rights" then being argued at a civil level and applied to the dioceses.

However, in 1868 a permissive canon was narrowly adopted allowing dioceses to federate within the same state. (WD, 326) An article was published two years later by Trinity Chapel New York advocating the mandatory organization of the church into such provinces. Several reasons were given for this action, including the need for appellate courts and the view that such dioceses would have common issues because of being within the same state. Specifically mentioned were the two New York dioceses working at odds with each other on modifications to the state's "incorporation of parishes" laws. (TPS, 6) The canon adopted in 1868 made all decisions of these state provinces subject to the approval of the General Convention.

At every subsequent General Convention until 1901 (which saw the adoption of Article VII allowing for a provincial system) the matter was discussed, often with great emotion. The House of Deputies Committee on the Constitution wrote in 1874:

> Any institution of Provinces or Provincial Synods with powers at all times subject to revocation by the General Convention, would be useless and illusory. The Provinces, if invested with irrevocable powers, and discharged from the constant and necessary authority and supervision of the General Convention, certainly might, and probably would, soon diverge into widely differing practices and opinions, engendering ecclesiastical conflicts threatening the unity of the church. (JGC 1874, 151)

Interestingly enough, one proposal which was defeated in 1895 would have created provinces not smaller than five contiguous dioceses each headed by an "Archbishop."

In 1901, Article VII of the constitution was adopted which gave the General Convention the ability to divide the church into geographic provinces. It would not be until 1913 that canons specifying how this was to be done would be adopted, when Canon 50 outlined the form and function of the provinces. The church was divided into eight provinces but no diocese could be made a part of a province without its consent. Each province was to have a provincial synod, which was essentially a legislative body. The president of the synod was to be one of the bishops, and each diocese was to be represented by four lay and four clerical deputies in addition to their bishop(s). The canon is long, comprised of eleven sections, and does not bear repeating in full here. However, section VI outlined the function of the provincial synod and is germane to our discussion:

> The provincial Synod when duly organized shall have power
>
> > (1) to enact ordinances for its own regulation and
> > Governance;

(2) to act as or provide for (a) a provincial Board of Missions
(b) a provincial board of Religious Education and (c) a
Provincial Board of Social Services, to be severally aux-
iliary to the General Boards having jurisdiction of the
subjects;

(3) to elect judges to the court of review;

(4) to perform other such duties as may be committed to it by
the General Convention;

(5) to deal with all matters within the province, provided
that no provincial Synod shall have power to regulate or
control the policy or internal affairs of any constituent
Diocese or Missionary Districts, and provided further that
all actions and proceedings of the Synod shall be subject to
and in conformity with the provisions of the Constitution
and Canons for the government of this church. (JGC
1901, 541)

In other words, the main function of the province was to enable
common ministry within its geographical area. While the provincial
synod was technically a legislative body, its power was limited to the
internal organization, mission, and ministry of the province and subject to General Convention. It was also clear that the province had no
authority over dioceses.

In 1919 General Convention formed a committee on the "Enlarged
Powers of the Provinces." The canon was substantially revised and
renumbered as Canon 53. Of greatest import was the grant of power to
"provide for the making of a survey of resources and needs, Provincial
and Diocesan, preceding the meeting of each General Convention,
for the presentation to the General Convention and provided for the
General Convention to refer matters to the Provincial Synods." (JGC
1919, 564-567, CC 1919, 139-140)

In 1922 the powers of the provincial synods were reworked. Although
the order and language are slightly different, the content is essentially
the same as the current canon (I.9.8), which reads:

The provincial Synod shall have power:

(a) to enact Ordinances for its own regulation and
government;

(b) to elect judges of the Provincial Court of Review

(c) to such duties as many (sic) be committed to it by the General Convention

(d) to deal with all matters within the province; *Provided, however,* that no Provincial Synod may have the power to regulate or control the internal policy or affairs of any constituent Diocese: and *Provided further,* that all actions and proceedings of the Synod shall be subject to and in conformity with the Constitution and the Canons for the Government of this Church;

(e) to adopt a budget for the maintenance of any Provincial work undertaken by the Synod, such budget to be raised in such manner as the Synod may determine;

(f) to create by Ordinance a provincial Council with power to administer and carry on such work as may be committed to it by the General Convention, or by the Presiding Bishop and Executive Council, or by the Synod of the Province.

Between 1922 and the present, most changes to the canons concerned the composition of the provinces. There are, however, two significant changes during that time which should be mentioned.

In 1964, the ninth province was created comprising mostly Spanish-speaking overseas dioceses.

In 1976, the canon was modified to allow for the president to be elected from any order, providing that, if the president were lay or clerical, the vice president be a bishop. This, in conjunction with House of Bishops General Rule XXVII, creates an interesting dynamic with regard to the Presiding Bishop's Council of Advice and the President of the House of Deputies' Council: while the President of the House of Deputies selects her Council of Advice, the Presiding Bishop's is made up of the bishops elected president or vice president by each of the provinces.

As the province relates to the Executive Council, it should be noted that in 1973 Canon I.4.1.c was amended to require each province to elect one lay and ordained member to Executive Council.

There has been much discussion both formally and informally about the effectiveness of the provinces. In 1971 the Standing Committee on Structure commissioned an independent study of the national structure of The Episcopal Church. Often referred to as the Booz-Allen Report after the firm which wrote it, it did not find that the provincial structure was very effective at any level. One section was entitled "Most Provinces Serve Little Apparent Purpose in the Church Today," in which it was stated that the provinces were not "fundamental to the work of the church" (58) and concluded that "...provinces lack the authority, budget, and staff, which are necessary to give any organization real purpose." (59) It ultimately recommended the dissolution of the system. This recommendation was rejected.

Currently, the effectiveness and functionality of each province is dependent on that province. Some are very active, meeting regularly, and some are not. What can be said is that the provinces provide a way to ensure that there is broad geographic representation on Executive Council and that the provincial system creates a mechanism for Executive Council to report back to the dioceses. The provinces also provide a court of appeals for ecclesiastical trials.

Besides these canonical purposes, the main advantage of the current provincial system may be communication and the exchange of ideas and information.

In that light, the most important meeting for any province may be the one which occurs immediately before the General Convention. Representatives of the General Convention staff, and often the Presiding Officers, attend the meeting to discuss important resolutions and to review the proposed triennial budget. The time and cost involved means that there is no way that this could be done on a diocese-by-diocese basis. Gathering the dioceses together in provinces for such General Convention previews allows bishops and deputies to be better informed when they arrive at General Convention.

As mentioned above, at each province meeting the provincial members of the Executive Council are to attend and are given time to brief the province members on the Council's work. Again, it would be difficult if not impossible to do this on a diocese-by-diocese basis. This also gives the members of the province an opportunity to provide input to Executive Council members, who in some way represent them to Council.

The networking aspect of provinces is also important. Provincial meetings provide an opportunity for members to share ministry ideas from their dioceses and parishes. It also opens the opportunity for dioceses to assist each other in such ministries. So for example, a diocese which has developed a strong youth ministry is available to assist a diocese struggling to create an effective ministry in this area. This is essentially what was envisioned by the convention of 1913 when it called for the provinces to create "boards" in various ministry areas. Now it is done in a more informal manner.

It seems clear that the provincial system has never reached the potential that many envisioned when it was instituted in the early twentieth century. It was thought that General Convention might delegate some of its responsibilities to the provinces (and this is still permitted by canon) but this rarely happens. There is an inherent tension in the powers of the provinces as noted by the General Convention report of 1874. Provinces which are subject in all things to the General Convention can get very little accomplished, while independent provinces would inevitably lead to a lack of uniformity in the wider church.

Yet the system remains and is useful to us as a vehicle for electing Courts of Review and Executive Council members. It also provides a means for communicating the work of the Executive Council and the General Convention and allows opportunities for dioceses to network around issues of mission and ministry.

The Development and Role of Executive Council

Charles Osberger

Canon 4: Of the Executive Council

There shall be an Executive Council of the General Convention whose
duty it shall be to carry out the programs and policies adopted by General
Convention. The Executive Council shall have charge of the coordination,
development and implementation of the ministry and mission of the Church.
(CC I.4.a)

An earlier author skillfully corrected a common misperception.
"Many persons have thought that the Executive Council is the governing body of the church and that the General Convention is the servant of the Council when in fact the opposite is true." (Wallace, 61)
General Convention created Executive Council and over many years
the relationship between both has evolved in significant ways.

How did Executive Council come to be? In what ways has Executive
Council developed in response to the will of General Convention?

This introduction to Executive Council seeks to explore how developments in the role of Council reflect our understanding of the representative nature of church governance, and the distributive manner in
which the church's mission is carried out.

Formative Years of Council

The National Council, forerunner to Executive Council, was
largely a twentieth century response to the growth in the number of

congregations and jurisdictions of The Episcopal Church at home and abroad, and the desire to organize the potential for mission in productive ways. Council came into being during an era of national enthusiasm led by corporations and governments to create efficient bureaucracies characterized by central control and planning. Support for these developments led to passage of a canon creating a central council, with a unified budget, and a more prominent role for the Presiding Bishop in leading mission program initiatives.

The Council came into existence in 1919 by virtue of Canon 60 entitled "Of the Presiding Bishop and Council" about which White and Dykman, in the *Annotated Constitution and Canons*, offer this explanation:

> There was...strong sentiment in the Church that there should be a co-ordination of the missionary, religious education and social service departments; and a closer relationship between the Presiding Bishop...and the several departments of the Church's work. (WD, 248)

On December 31, 1919, three independent boards (the Board of Missions of the Domestic and Foreign Missionary Society, the General Board of Religious Education and the Social Services Commission) were replaced by the new entity called, "the Presiding Bishop and Council."

The Council was constituted with 24 members, sixteen elected by General Convention (four bishops, four presbyters, and eight lay persons). The provincial synods each elected one representative to Council. There were also provisions to elect a first and second vice president, secretary and treasurer of the Domestic and Foreign Missionary Society (DFMS) serving as the treasurer of National Council.

Because of Council's relationship to the Board of The Domestic and Foreign Missionary Society of The Protestant Episcopal Church (DFMS), a paragraph about this relationship might be helpful.

> As early as 1808, the subject of domestic missions was considered in General Convention, when a committee appointed to address the Church at large on certain matters was "authorized and desired to consider and determine on the proper mode of sending a Bishop in said States and Territories," meaning thereby

those states and territories in which the Church was not yet organized. (WD, 209)

The DFMS was established in 1821. All persons who are members
of the church were considered members of the Society. In the first
few years of its existence, the church gave meager support to its missionary work, and it was not until 1835 that the church awoke to its
responsibilities. The General Convention of that year enunciated two
great principles: first, reaffirming the original articles that every baptized member of the church was a member of the Society and second
that the whole world was its field of work. Significant new funding
under the banner of the National Campaign advanced these principles. The DFMS was incorporated in 1846 in the State of New York.
The Board of the Society, being the first incorporated national body of
"The Protestant Episcopal Church in the United States of America,"
(PECUSA)[18] retained the corporate name of the church. As noted above
the Convention of 1919 assumed responsibility for the whole work of
the church including the Board of the DFMS. Article II of the Society
constituted the Executive Council (National Council) as its Board of
Directors.[19]

The General Convention of 1919 was also the first to call for the
election of a Presiding Bishop, revising the previous process of allot-
ting this office by seniority within the House of Bishops. In 1926, John
Gardner Murray of Maryland became the first Presiding Bishop to
be elected. The Council created five departments (the equivalent of
today's standing committees). The bylaws provided that the Presiding
Bishop serve as the chief executive and chair, *ex officio*, of each depart-
ment. The Presiding Bishop was given power to appoint one of the
two vice presidents to serve the National Council.

Transformation and Authority

The General Convention of 1934 revised the Presiding Bishop's role
on Council. Although the Presiding Bishop would continue to serve as
ex officio chair of the National Council and to preside at meetings when

---

[18] The two acronyms combined represent the full official title of the corporation.

[19] For more on the history of the DFMS and its role in the mission of the church, see Ian Douglas' 1996 study, *Fling Out the Banner: The National Church Ideal and the Foreign Mission of the Episcopal Church*. (New York: The Church Hymnal Corporation.)

present, the vice-chair was to be elected by the House of Deputies. The concept of Presiding Bishop as chief executive officer was evolving. Governance diminished as a key responsibility and was replaced by a primary focus on the prosecution of the church's mission.

General Convention (1964) renamed National Council the "Executive Council." Multiple departmental committees compiled an impressive record of initiatives and accomplishments. But centralization was also perceived to have created an unwieldy bureaucracy unresponsive to the changing social climate of the 1960s. The composition of Council, its representative nature, was highly influenced by currents of social change, especially governance roles for women, lay persons, and the inclusion of African-American Episcopalians.

Questions of authority and levels of authority were brought poignantly into the open in the early 1960s. In response to a pastoral letter by Presiding Bishop Lichtenberger, the House of Bishops proposed a resolution in the form of a statement, "The Levels of Authority within the Church." This resolution identified four levels of authority within The Episcopal Church: (1) Scripture, the Creeds, the BCP, Constitution and Canons, and the resolutions and statements of General Convention; (2) the House of Bishops; (3) the Presiding Bishop and Executive Council; and (4) the officers and staff of the Executive Council. The Presiding Bishop and Executive Council were charged with representing the church and implementing the decisions of the General Convention, and—given the pace of world events between meetings of General Convention—vested with a distinctive role to "speak God's word to his Church and his world."

Leading to General Convention 1967, Presiding Bishop Hines appointed a Mutual Responsibility Commission looking specifically at the relationship between the Presiding Bishop, General Convention and Executive Council. This Commission presented an expansive view of Council as acting for General Convention between sessions—a view that did not prevail, in part due to concerns that Council could displace the historic role of General Convention.

Convention chose rather to adopt revisions to Canon 4 that restated Council's role, "in charge of the unification, development and prosecution of the missionary, educational and social work of the Church, and any such other work as may be committed by General Convention." This is the substance of today's Canon I.4.

The Standing Commission on Structure, in advance of General Convention 1976, once again revisited the concepts of governance related to structure. Key to its report is the reaffirmation of The Episcopal Church as a representative body.

> The Church, as an organization, is basically a democracy divinely motivated and led. Its democratic nature is defined by the way in which it functions and, by its functioning, establishes the responsibility and authority of the different organizational components.

The Presiding Bishop and the Executive Council acting together form the administrative or executive (non-legislative) arm of the General Convention and are responsible for carrying out the programs and policy adopted by the General Convention. The relationship between the Presiding Bishop and Executive Council was defined as "yoked together" to share "(to the extent they can be shared) the burdens and responsibility of administration." Council and the Presiding Bishop are the principle links to provinces and dioceses between Conventions.

Efforts continue to realign commissions, committees and task forces in a coherent whole that serves the mission of the church. Motions to limit the number, scope, and charge of commissions have been adopted in recent decades. At the center of these proposals is the belief in a structure of governance maintaining the widest possible participation for witness and action, balanced with concerns for efficiency and cost-effectiveness.

Commissions and Structure

Executive Council is vital to this effort, in naming a liaison to each of the standing commissions of the General Convention. In addition, there are five Standing Committees of Executive Council: The Joint Standing Committee on Finances for Mission, the Joint Standing Committee on Governance and Administration for Mission, the Standing Committee on Local Ministry and Mission (local being the congregational level), the Standing Committee on Advocacy and Networking for Mission (addressing concerns at the church-wide level), and the Standing Committee on World Mission (addressing concerns outside The Episcopal Church). The President of the House of Deputies is vice-chair of Council and vice president of the Board of the DFMS, and the Board itself is formed by the Executive Council membership. The Presiding Bishop also appoints a member of her staff to serve as liaison to each standing commission and standing committee.Membership of (Joint) Standing Committees is jointly appointed by the chair and vice-chair of Executive Council. Council elects this church's members of the Anglican Consultative Council (ACC) and other Anglican and ecumenical bodies for which no other procedure is provided.

Council is required by canon to meet at least three times each year. Council is charged with the responsibility to submit to General Convention the triennial budget for The Episcopal Church. The draft proposed budget is prepared by Council and handed over to the Joint Standing Committee on Program, Budget and Finance, which offers a final proposed budget to the General Convention. This budget provides for the canonical, corporate and program expenses of the church, including costs associated with General Convention. In its capacity as the Board of the DFMS, Council is invested with power to direct the funds available from the Society for the mission of the church. Council may amend the budget between Conventions but is limited to the total budget revenues adopted by Convention.

Executive Council is presently composed of:

(a) Twenty members: four bishops, four clergy (presbyters or deacons) and twelve laity elected by General Convention for a six year term.

(b) Eighteen members: one bishop or presbyter and one lay person elected by Provincial Synods, also serving a six year term.

(c) *Ex officio* members are the Presiding Bishop as chair, and the President of the House of Deputies as vice-chair.

(d) The Secretary and Treasurer of Council are accorded seat and voice but no vote.

Discerning the Future: Closing Points

- We have affirmed, from the earliest days of General Convention, a form of governance that embodies and involves the whole church. The beginnings of Executive Council demonstrate this principle of representation and involvement.

- We have affirmed the relevance of all orders of ministry sharing in the governance of this church, and the Executive Council structure reflects this commitment to making use of the gifts of members of the church in all orders.

- We have made productive use of the tensions and challenges in our history in order better to adapt our structures for the work of the church.

- We are responding as a church to the witness of the Spirit who calls us into mission.

The Presiding Officers

Jim Simons

The President of the House of Deputies

There is scant information available about the development of the role of the President of the House of Deputies over the course of our history. There is no doubt, however, that there have been significant changes in the office since the first General Convention. The position has grown from a mere presiding officer early in the church's history to a spokesperson and representative of The Episcopal Church nationally and internationally.

When the first General Convention was convened in Philadelphia in 1785 it was obvious to the small assembly that they would need a Presiding Officer. William White, then rector at Christ Church Philadelphia, was elected by the House of Deputies.[20] His role was to preside over the meeting of the Convention and at its close his duties were ended.

Canons regarding the General Convention didn't mention the office of President until 1904. In that year Canon 46 was adapted from the first Rule of Order for the House of Deputies passed in 1841 (and printed on the obverse of the Title Page of the Journal for that Convention). The Rule, simply entitled "Order," outlined the process for the organization of the General Convention. In the House of Deputies, the meeting was called to order by the Secretary and after the deputies

---

[20] There was no House of Bishops at General Convention until 1789, at which point by-then-bishop William White would be its presiding officer. (Barnes, 52)

were certified and a quorum established the first item of business was the election of the President of the House. The rule adopted would seem to have simply codified the practice that the House had employed informally at previous Conventions. (CC 1904, 109) This was the practice until 1964.

The canons for the General Convention in place prior to this address the role of the Secretary of the House, the Treasurer, and Registrar, but not the President. It could be speculated that the reason for the absence of mention of the President was the obvious need for one and the confinement of the role to presiding over the House of Deputies when the Convention was convened. Unlike the other officers, the President had no other responsibilities, roles, or duties.

This practice of electing the President at the beginning of Convention prevailed until 1964 when the Canon was changed to provide for the election of the next President during Convention. (JGC 1964, 222-223) The term of office began with the close of the electing Convention. This was done to allow the President to appoint members of Convention committees in advance of the next Convention. The first President so elected was Clifford Morehouse, a lay leader from the Diocese of New York. (JGC 1964, 164) It would appear that this changed the House's perception of the role of the President. Before 1964 the perception was that the President was elected for each Convention alone. With the canonical changes the President was now understood to be the President for the triennium, through the next Convention. This shifted the role of the President, and assigned more responsibility between Conventions.

It would seem that there had also been a longstanding assumption that the President would be from the clerical order (TPS, 9). Although the 1841 rule of order and the canon of 1909 provided that the President of the House of Deputies be elected from "its members," no layperson was elected to the office until 1946. In that year the Honorable Owen Josephus Roberts, a retired Federal Supreme Court justice from the Diocese of Pennsylvania, was elected. In the sixty-five years to follow only four other lay people have held the office. Clifford Morehouse 1961, 64, 67; Dr. Charles Lawrence (the only African-American to hold the office) 1979, 82, 85; Dr. Pamela Chinnis 1994, 97, 2000; and Dr. Bonnie Anderson 2009, 12.

1964 was also the year that the office of Vice-President was introduced. Until this office was introduced the Secretary was charged with filling in for a deceased or disabled President. The first Vice-President of the House was the Very Rev. John C. Leffler of Olympia. (JGC 1964, 165) Every sitting Vice-President has succeeded the outgoing President since Dr. Charles Lawrence succeeded the Very Rev. John Coburn at the conclusion of the 1976 Convention. (Collins, 267) Canon 1.1.1.b also required that the President and Vice-President be of different orders. It is also interesting that since 1946, when the first layperson was elected President, that succeeding Presidents have alternated between lay and ordained. The exception to this is The Rev. Theodore Wedel who succeeded Dean Clyde Sprouse in 1952, in difficult and unusual circumstances: Dean Sprouse collapsed on the platform shortly after being elected and died of a heart attack. (JGC 1952, 94)

The President is *ex officio* a member of the House. This means that while the President of the House must be elected from among the deputies it is not necessary that the President be a deputy at the next Convention over which he or she presides. This has happened twice in recent memory, with Dean David Collins in 1991 and Dean George Werner in 2006.

In 1967 what is now Canon I.1.2 was adopted. It outlined procedures for the appointment of interim bodies. Until this time they were prescribed by the Rules of Order. The President of the House of Deputies appoints all of the lay and clerical deputies to these commissions and is (as is the Presiding Bishop) an *ex officio* member of every commission. (WD, 170) That same year Canon 4 (now Canon I.3) was changed to make the Presiding Bishop Chairman (now President), and the President of the House of Deputies Vice Chair (now Vice President), of DFMS. The President of the House of Deputies is also an *ex officio* member of all Executive Council standing committees.

The President of the House of Deputies is also responsible for assigning members of the House to convention legislative committees. She may seek to do this with the help of her Council of Advice, which she appoints. (This is in contrast to the Presiding Bishop's Council of Advice which is constituted of the Provincial Presidents or Vice Presidents who are bishops). In both the case of interim bodies and

Convention committees the President seeks to strike a balance in areas such as gender, ethnicity, geography, and theological perspective.

Also in 1967, the term of office for the President and Vice-President was prescribed. Neither shall serve in that position for more than three consecutive three year terms. Canon I.1.b specifies that if the President is unable to perform her duties that the Vice-President assumes the role. However, one of the apparent gaps in our current canons is the lack of a process to replace the Vice-President should a vacancy occur in that office between Conventions. This was the case between the 1991 and 1994 as well as the 2009 and 2012 conventions.

It is arguable that the changes in 1967 forever altered the office of President of the House of Deputies and perhaps the pool of candidates who are willing or able to hold the office. This is in part due to the fact that, unlike the Presiding Bishop, the President of the House of Deputies does not receive a salary. This means that the individual holding the position must have some source of income, and plentiful available time. Given the schedule that recent Presidents have maintained and the demands upon their schedule, it is unlikely that anyone would be able to fill the position while holding a full-time job elsewhere. The last President to hold the office while still holding full-time employment was Dean John Coburn who was the Rector of St. James Church in New York City and Bishop-elect of Massachusetts during his last convention in 1976. Since then, every President has either been retired or in a position where they did not need to be employed.

Until the late seventies the President of the House of Deputies presided over the House at Convention, attended Executive Council meetings and some interim body meetings. However, over the past twenty-five years the Presidents of the House have maintained a much higher profile nationally and internationally. Recent Presidents have made a concerted effort to be involved with the work of all interim bodies as well as Executive Council and its committees. This is an enormous time commitment as there are approximately twenty-five such committees and commissions involved. Also, recent Presidents have responded to invitations to numerous events such as diocesan conventions, and seminary lectures and graduations. As our understanding of our connectedness to the wider Anglican Communion has grown over the past decades, so have invitations for the President to travel to other provinces to bring and receive hope and encouragement. The role of President has come to include being a spokesperson for The Episcopal Church both at home and abroad

Over the years, the role of the President of the House of Deputies has evolved from being completely unmentioned in the canons for the first 125 years of the church to being a dynamic and vital participant in the life and governance of The Episcopal Church and The Anglican Communion. We have been well served by a variety of faithful men and women, lay and ordained, who dedicated themselves to the service of the church. Each brought their own gifts and talents and shaped their Presidency in a unique way. All have been an encouragement and blessing to the House.

The Authority of the Office of the Presiding Bishop

The purpose of this essay is to consider the history of and to describe the current state of the authority of the office of the Presiding Bishop. While the history of the office will be considered, the scope of this reflection will not allow a detailed rehearsal of all its aspects. There are, however, several excellent and accessible resources which a give a detailed accounting of that history. Among them are

> *The Role of the Presiding Bishop*, by Roland Foster (1982)
> *Changes in the Structure, Organization, and Government of The Episcopal Church in the Last Sixty Years*, by the Rev. Canon Charles Guilbert (1982)
> *The Study and Development of the Office of The Presiding Bishop*, by William Joseph Barnds (1958)
> *The Roles, Duties and Responsibilities of the Executive Council, Domestic and Foreign Missionary Society, Presiding Bishop and President of the House of Deputies in the Governance of The Episcopal Church*, by Robert C. Royce, Esq. (2009).

All are available from the Archives of The Episcopal Church, the staff of which have been invaluable in producing this reflection.[21]

---

[21] For much of this paper the masculine is used when referring to the Presiding Bishop. This is simply reflective of all but recent history, and of the materials consulted and their implicit assumptions that the Presiding Bishop would be male. In the conclusion I use the feminine to reflect the current reality.

1789–1919

For over a century, beginning with The Episcopal Church's organizational birth in 1789, the Presiding Bishop was primarily seen as the Presiding Officer of the House of Bishops. Although duties evolved within that period, initially they were essentially to preside over the House of Bishops and to preside at the consecration of new bishops, which generally happened at the General Convention. A further clarification on this role of presiding was in place in Article III of the 1789 Constitution; this stated that the House of Bishops could not meet as a body unless there were three bishops present. When there were fewer than three, they were to sit with their deputations in the House of Deputies with the provision that a bishop "shall preside" over the unicameral body. This is perhaps the first foreshadowing of the Presiding Bishop's office evolving into the role of leadership for the whole church, rather than simply as presiding officer of the House of Bishops.

The General Convention of 1799 was the first to convey specific duties to the Presiding Bishop by assigning the authority to call special meetings of the General Convention. Other responsibilities were added by subsequent General Conventions, including reviewing consents for elections of bishops and being the President of the "The Protestant Episcopal Missionary Society in the United States." (Barnds, 257)

However, as late as 1832, the term "Presiding Bishop" was used in a somewhat fluid way as the House of Bishops passed a rule that the senior bishop present at any House of Bishops' meeting was the Presiding Bishop, and, at a consecration, the senior bishop present would be the "presiding bishop." (Perry, 146)

Until 1926, the Presiding Bishop was the senior bishop in order of consecration. This may have worked well when the church was smaller and the duties of the Presiding Bishop minimal, but as the office evolved, and The Episcopal Church grew, the burden placed on one who was often the oldest member of the House became increasingly unreasonable. This, coupled with the fact that there was no provision for the Presiding Bishop to resign, made the situation increasingly intolerable. As early as 1836 criticism of the system was voiced by the Presiding Bishop himself: Alexander Griswold questioned the wisdom of such an arrangement, which often meant the Presiding Bishop was far from the geographic center of the church (Griswold was in the Eastern Diocese which comprised most of New England) and further, stated that "those duties will often fall upon one, who, by reason of old age, is least capable of performing them." (Stone, 404)

In the early years of the church, Pastoral Letters were often written by the Presiding Bishop acting alone. In an 1836 letter to Bishop Onderdonk, Presiding Bishop Griswold declined to do this and suggested that the House of Bishops form a committee to do so in the future. This practice continues today. (Stone, 404)

1919–1964

The General Convention of 1919 was a watershed for the way in which The Episcopal Church saw and structured itself. Edwin Augustine White, in his seminal work *Constitution and Canons*, commented

> Canon 60 [now Canon I.4, "Of The Executive Council"] with the amendments made by the Convention of 1922, undoubtedly marks a greater change in the polity of The Episcopal Church than any other Canon ever enacted by the General Convention and is one of the greatest pieces of constructive legislation, if not the greatest, ever enacted by that body since the first General Convention of 1789.

> The Church began her National life with practically no executive head, and no central governing power, save only the General Convention, meeting once in three years, and whose functions were chiefly legislative, not executive.

> ...As she began, so she continued in great measure for one hundred and thirty years, until the General Convention of 1919, when in one fell swoop she discarded all her past traditions in the manner of executive government, and by enactment of Canon 60, erected a strong form of centralized government. To one central body the Church committed the administration of her work, giving to the Presiding Bishop and the National Council [now Executive Council]...not only the performance of such work as the General Convention may commit to that body, but also the power to initiate and develop such new work as it may deem necessary...the Presiding Bishop and the National Council

are restricted only by the provisions of the Constitution and Canons and such directions as may be given to it by the General Convention; but outside of these restrictions, there is a large field in which the Presiding Bishop and Council may act, unhampered by any restraints. (White 1924, 958-959)

This commentary has been echoed in both revised editions of the *Annotated Constitution and Canons*. (WD 1954, 244-245; WD 1982, 271-272)

Among the resolutions the General Convention passed were canons providing for the election of the Presiding Bishop, setting an age-limit for service, term of office, and making the Presiding Bishop President of the National Council (now Executive Council).

Perhaps most significant was the introduction of Canon 16 (now I.2.4), which described the duties of the Presiding Bishop. It read:

> The Presiding Bishop shall preside over the House of Bishops, and shall take order for the consecration of Bishops, when duly elected; *and he shall be the Executive Head of all departments of the Church's work, including those of Missions and Church Extension, of Religious Education and Christian Social Service.* He shall also perform all other duties prescribed for him by other Canons of this General Convention. (*Emphasis added.*)

For the first time in the polity of the church, the Presiding Bishop was given executive authority. However, this would be short-lived. The convention of 1922 removed the text that appears in italics above. This canon would then remain unchanged until 1967. (WD, 200)

The "work" described in this canon seems to represent the three major ministry groups of the time (The Board of Missions, The General Board of Religious Education, and the Commission for Social Service), which were united into the National Council and of which the Presiding Bishop was the President. (Guilbert, 24) It may be tempting to see the removal of the language in 1922 as an attempt to remove redundancy. However, it would also seem that there is a significant difference between "Executive Head of all Departments" and "President of Council." It would appear that this was an intentional move on the part of General Convention to reduce these new untested powers of the Presiding Bishop and move toward a more collegial form of governance and executive action.

However, the Convention of 1919 did move the church toward a more centralized, corporate understanding of itself, and the Presiding Bishop's office would no longer be the same.

The second major change during this period was with regard to the diocesan responsibilities of the Presiding Bishop. As the work of the Presiding Bishop grew it became increasingly unreasonable to be both a diocesan bishop and Presiding Bishop. However, up until this point no Primate in the Anglican Communion was without a See.

The Convention of 1907 began to provide some relief by passing a constitutional change (Article I.3), which allowed the diocese from which the Presiding Bishop was elected immediately to elect a bishop coadjutor to handle whatever responsibilities seemed advisable to the newly elected Presiding Bishop. (1907 JGC, 342)

By 1937, this constitutional provision had become a canonical one and the canon was changed to make the election of a coadjutor mandatory for the affected diocese and required the Presiding Bishop to assign the coadjutor such responsibility "as will relieve the Presiding Bishop from all duties in the diocese which will necessitate his presence therein." (JGC 1937, 439)

The transition was completed in 1943 when Canon 18 was passed, requiring a bishop, upon election as Presiding Bishop, to resign his see and jurisdiction. (Foster, 93)

During this period, it is obvious that the role of the Presiding Bishop was changing informally as well. In 1937, "The Joint Committee on Status and Work of the Presiding Bishop" issued a report which suggested that it would be unwise for the General Convention to specifically define the role of the Presiding Bishop. Rather, the Joint Committee postulated that it was best to let each Presiding Bishop shape the role for himself, observing that, "Granted an office of this sort, the men chosen for it will themselves create its traditions." (JGC 1937, 488)

At the same time, the Joint Committee was very clear that the Presiding Bishop's role was becoming—and needed to be—vested with more symbolism. They wrote,

> ...We would say that this church needs, increasingly, a vis-
> ible symbol of its National unity.... No committee like the
> National Council, nor any large assemblage, like the General
> Convention...can ever be as truly symbolic as an individual
> leader. This accords with the facts of human nature and with the
> central truth of the Christian religion—the Incarnation of the
> Son of God. (JGC 1937, 488)

The office of Presiding Bishop was now moving from the low-pro-
file practical roles and understandings it carried in the 1800s both to a
more corporate and more symbolic understanding. The role's emphasis
had shifted from one of serving as the presiding officer of the House of
Bishops to being the corporate and symbolic leader of The Episcopal
Church.

Still, the only description of the duties of the Presiding Bishop
between 1922 and 1964 was to be found in Canon I.2.4 (changed from
Canon 16 in 1943) which read:

> The Presiding Bishop shall preside over meetings of the House
> of Bishops, and shall take order for the consecration of Bishops,
> when duly elected. He shall also perform all other duties pre-
> scribed for him by other canons of the General Convention.

1964–Present

While historians often comment on the seismic shift in the church's
polity following the Convention of 1919, the General Convention of
1967 may have been just as significant for the church's understanding
of the role of the Presiding Bishop.

In 1963 a discussion arose in the House of Bishops regarding individuals' speaking on behalf of the church. As we have seen, the church
had grown significantly, and, meanwhile the question, "Who speaks
for The Episcopal Church?" had never been settled by the General
Convention.

The Committee on Social and International Affairs proposed a resolution in the form of a statement entitled "Levels of Authority within
the Church." (JGC 1963, 312–313) It sought to clarify where authority
lay, by outlining four levels in a descending order:

1. The Protestant Episcopal Church accepts as its authority the Holy Scriptures, the Nicene and Apostles' Creeds, and speaks through the Book of Common Prayer and the Constitution and Canons of the Church. The Protestant Episcopal Church speaks also through the Resolutions, Statements, and actions of the General Convention. In these ways the Church speaks at the highest level of responsibility for the Church, to the Church and to the world.

2. Similarly, the House of Bishops, as the Fathers in God of the Church, speaks corporately to the Church the mind of its Chief Pastors. Further, each Bishop may speak as an apostolic Shepherd within his own jurisdiction, yet with a sense of mutual responsibility to his episcopal brethren and with faithfulness to the teaching of the Church.

3. In the interim of General Convention, the Presiding Bishop and the Executive Council are the responsible representatives of the Church, granted authority to implement the statements and actions of General Convention and of the House of Bishops. When, in the course of the fast-moving events of life today, it is not possible to await a meeting of General Convention, it is the duty of the Presiding Bishop and the Executive Council to speak God's word to his Church and to his world.

4. At a lesser level of responsibility and authority, the officers and staff of the Executive Council may, from time to time, speak their own Christian mind, after consultation with the Presiding Bishop, in areas of great concern in which General Convention has not acted. Such statements or actions should not be interpreted as the will of the whole Church, but as that of the individuals and group directly responsible.

It is level three which has the greatest relevance to the concerns of this essay. Several aspects of this four-level authority structure should be noted. Firstly, the order of authority vested in persons or organizations is basically (1) General Convention, (2) the House of Bishops, and (3) the Presiding Bishop and Executive Council. It seems clear that the Presiding Bishop's authority to speak for the church is presented as subservient to the General Convention and the House of Bishops.

Secondly, the precise meaning of "The Presiding Bishop and Executive Council" seems to be unclear. Does this mean that the Presiding Bishop and the Executive Council are separate but equal authorities in the church, or does the statement imply that they work cooperatively in speaking for the church? Given the Resolution's seeming reluctance to vest too much authority in any one person, it is most probably the latter interpretation which was intended, and such is the interpretation of commentators. (WD, 207)

Thirdly, the primary responsibility of the Presiding Bishop and Executive Council is to "implement the statements and actions of the General Convention." Only when a matter of some urgency arises and it is not possible to wait to address the concern until the next Convention may they speak on behalf of the church on such matters. They were not granted *carte blanche* to speak on any and every topic they might choose.

Of course, it will be noted that this was a resolution of Convention and the binding force of such resolutions has been debated.[22] However, it certainly reflected the mind of the General Convention at that time as it sought to clarify levels of authority and who it was who could speak on behalf of the church and has continued essentially unchanged as practice since that time.

In 1967, Canon I.2.4 was greatly expanded and for the first time duties of the Presiding Bishop (other than presiding at the House of Bishops and consecrations) were enumerated in one place.

Most significant were sub-sections (a) 1 and 2.

> (a) The Presiding Bishop shall be the chief pastor thereof. As such he shall
>
>> (1) Be charged with the responsibility for giving leadership in initiating and developing the policy and strategy of the Church;
>>
>> (2) Speak God's word to the Church and to the world, as the chief representative of this Church and its episcopate in its corporate capacity.

Several items are significant. First, the Presiding Bishop is now termed "chief pastor."[23] The Mutual Responsibility Commission, which proposed the change in the canon, was clear in their report to the General

---

[22] See the Note at the end of this chapter.

[23] As an interesting aside, the term was originally capitalized but changed to lower case during debate in the House of Deputies (JGC 1967, 322). The capitalization was restored in 1982.

Convention that they were indicating that the Presiding Bishop was to be the chief pastor for the *whole* church. No longer was he simply a presiding officer for one House: now he was given pastoral responsibility for the entire Episcopal Church. (JGC 1967, 256)

Second, the Presiding Bishop is now responsible for leading the initiation and development of policy and strategy. It is interesting that this canon seems to place the sole authority for this with the Presiding Bishop. However, the 1964 "Levels of Authority" resolution set the groundwork for an understanding of this issue, and in 1976 what was implicit (that this was to be exercised with Executive Council) was made explicit.

Third, the Presiding Bishop is now specifically authorized to speak God's word "to the Church and to the world" and to do so as its "chief representative."

Only three years earlier, when describing who had authority to speak for the church, the Presiding Bishop was listed third after the General Convention and The House of Bishops and only then in conjunction with the Executive Council. It would seem that this canon would promote the Presiding Bishop to the top of the priority list. However, this is not the establishment of some form of authority over the General Convention. It is clear from the Constitution and Canons that General Convention sets the course for the church and the expectation is that the Presiding Bishop will function as a chief executive acting as a spokesperson, whose statements will be consistent with those decisions. The dynamic being addressed is the limitations imposed due to the fact that the General Convention meets only every three years, and in a fast changing world someone must be authorized to speak for the church in the interim.

In 1976, subsection (1) was expanded so that after "Church" it continued:

> ...and as Chairman of the Executive Council of General Convention, with ultimate responsibility for implementation of such policy and strategy through the conduct of policies and programs authorized by the General Convention or approved by the Executive Council of the General Convention.

As stated above, this took the implied understanding that responsibility for initiatives and strategy were to be done in conjunction with the Executive Council and made it explicit in the canon. The report of the Legislative Committee on Structure specifically states this. (JGC 1976, AA-14)

In 1982, the Standing Commission on the Structure of the Church recommended that the Constitution be changed so that everywhere the phrase "Presiding Bishop" occurred it would be changed to "Archbishop." If this passed, then the changes would be made to the canons concurrent with the second reading on the constitutional change in 1985, when a new Presiding Bishop would be elected. In its report to the General Convention the Structure Commission wrote about this change:

> This [change] implies no change of his authority or any archiepis-copal jurisdiction, as is associated with other Christian bodies. It simply puts the Presiding Bishop on a par with other Anglican metropolitans, and clearly identifies his role as chief pastor of the church. (BB 1982, 340)

It is interesting that such a suggestion would be made. The Commission used several documents in its considerations including Bishop of St. Andrews John W.A. Howe's reflections on the nature of metropolitan authority. That document lists eight duties of a metropolitan and at the time of the Structure Report, the Presiding Bishop had only three of these.

Apparently, the idea of the Presiding Bishop being an Archbishop in name only was not well received by the Convention (or at least the House of Bishops). The concern at General Convention was that what would start out as a mere name-change would eventually lead to a substantive change and slide towards greater metropolitical authority.

The resolution was substituted on the floor of the House of Bishops. (JGC 1982, B42) No longer was it a resolution to change the Constitution, rather, it became a resolution to change Canon I.2.4.a so that it would now read:

> The Presiding Bishop of the Church shall be the Chief Pastor and Primate thereof...

Again the intention of the change was not substantially to alter the duties of the Presiding Bishop, but to give the office parity with other leaders of the Communion with regard to title.

The final substantive change (for our purposes) came in 1997. The Standing Commission on the Structure of the Church offered a wide range of Resolutions seeking to reduce the work of the church at its national level. Using the principle of subsidiarity, it sought to focus the work of the church best carried out at those levels in the parishes and dioceses. (BB 1997, 486)

This, in theory, was to reduce the administrative load of both the Executive Council and the Presiding Bishop. In addition, the Commission recommended that the ultimate responsibility for the implementation of the policies of the church be vested in the Executive Council with the Presiding Bishop as its President.

Canon I.2.4.a.1 was changed to state that the Presiding Bishop: "Be charged with the responsibility for leadership in initiating and developing the policy and strategy in the church and speaking for the church as to the policies, strategies and programs authorized by the General Convention." This is as the Canon reads today.

It would appear that while the Structure Commission wanted the Presiding Bishop to take on a more prophetic role and wanted to shift responsibilities from managing to leading (BB 1997, 486), it did so within what would seem to some to be narrow parameters. The Presiding Bishop is to function as spokesperson for the policies, strategies and programs authorized by the General Convention, and is responsible for a clear role of leadership in forming those policies and strategies.

Conclusions

The polity of The Episcopal Church differs in many ways from that of other provinces of the Anglican Communion. From its inception, the participation of laity and clergy in decision-making was a hallmark of our governance. No one person, or even body, except for General Convention, has been granted the authority to make decisions regarding the official policies of The Episcopal Church.

As the resolution of 1964 stated, there are four levels of authority in the church with the General Convention second only to Holy

Scripture, the Constitution and Canons, the Creeds, and *The Book of Common Prayer,* in the hierarchy of authority. General Convention has the final say in the amendment of two out of four of these "higher-level" authorities, as the law and liturgy (the Doctrine, Discipline and Worship) of the church are in its care. It is the General Convention which sets the direction, priorities, and policies of The Episcopal Church.

The Episcopal Church has explicitly rejected the idea of an Archbishop (even in name only) or of full archiepiscopal or metropolitical authority for the Presiding Bishop[24], seeking instead to continue with a polity of shared authority and decision-making within and under the General Convention. The Presiding Bishop's explicit responsibilities appear in various places throughout the Canons.

In 1901, Presiding Bishop Clark, in his convention address, remarked:

> There is nowhere to be found any general statement whatever of the duties pertaining to the office, and as it requires a careful examination of the Canons in order to ascertain just what it is that the Presiding Bishop is called upon to do, may I be allowed to suggest that some statement be set forth clearly defining the functions and duties of the office. (Foster 51)

It wouldn't be until sixty-six years later that any sort of statement was placed in the canons which described the function of the office beyond presiding at the House of Bishops and taking order for consecrations.

The statement as it appears today in Canon I.2.4 defines the role as Chief Pastor and Primate. As Chief Pastor she is to minister to the whole church in much the same way as a rector would interact pastorally with her congregation. This would tend to imply some sense of political and perhaps even theological neutrality as the Presiding Bishop recognizes the breadth of diversity in The Episcopal Church. The title Primate, as we have seen, was introduced in 1982 in order to give parity of name with the rest of the worldwide Anglican Communion, and implies no authority beyond that which the Canons allow.

---

[24] While the Presiding Bishop is not a metropolitan in the full sense of the word, most particularly in not having jurisdiction over a metropolitical see, some of the duties and powers of the Presiding Bishop are the same as some of those exercised by a metropolitan, including: visitation of dioceses (I.2.4.a.6), calling meetings of the House of Bishops as a Council (I.2.4.a.5), issuing Pastoral Letters (I.2.4.b), commissioning bishops for congregations overseas (I.15.7), holding the final power to dispense members of nationally recognized Religious Orders and other Christian Communities from their vows (III.14.1.d and 2.d), and numerous responsibilities related to church discipline.

Jackson A. Dykman wrote in 1954[25] of the office of the Presiding Bishop:

> The office of Presiding Bishop is a constitutional office, the tenure and duties of which are prescribed by the canons of General Convention and he has no duties or powers save as are so prescribed. . . . In other words, he has no traditional or common law duties such as may reside in a diocesan. (WD 1954, 176)

The Presiding Bishop is also to lead and develop policy and strategy. However, this is not policy and strategy created *ex nihilo* by the Presiding Bishop; rather, these policies and strategies, if not initiated by the General Convention, must at least be in concert with the policies and strategies of that body.

Finally, the Presiding Bishop is a spokesperson for the policies, strategies, and programs of the General Convention. It is her responsibility to represent to the wider church and to the world what the Convention has accomplished and initiated.

However, there remains another, more intangible, aspect of the office. As Robert Royce wrote in 2009:

> Viewing Presiding Bishops from Sherrill to Lichtenberger to Hines to Allin to Browning and Griswold, an observer would see vastly different understandings, activities and approaches to the role of a Presiding Bishop.

As we have seen, the General Convention of 1937 received a report regarding the role of the Presiding Bishop in which it was stated that it may not be to the advantage of the church to be too specific about the office of Presiding Bishop. Instead, those who inhabit it will "shape its traditions."

Each of the twenty-five individuals (William White was Presiding Bishop two different times) brought a unique character to the office. Force of personality and distinct interests make each administration different even within the same canonical confines.

While debate continues as to the scope of the role of the Presiding Bishop, and while different personalities shape the office uniquely, the roles of Chief Pastor, Primate, Leader, and Spokesperson are the integral keys to this ministry.

---

[25] This statement was retained by the editors in the current edition. (WD, 203-204).

A Table of Presiding Officers

Note: Barnes lists all of the Presidents of the House of Deputies and Presiding Bishops up to 1950. A detailed record of all of the Presiding Bishops appears in The Church Annual.

Presidents of the House of Deputies since 1952

1952	The Very Rev. Claude W. Sprouse (died minutes after being elected)
	The Rev. Canon Theodore Wedel
1955	The Rev. Canon Theodore Wedel
1958	The Rev. Canon Theodore Wedel
1961	Clifford Morehouse
1964	Clifford Morehouse
1967	Clifford Morehouse
1969	(special convention) The Rev. John Coburn
1970	The Rev. John Coburn
1973	The Rev. John Coburn
1976	The Rev. John Coburn
1979	Dr. Charles Lawrence
1982	Dr. Charles Lawrence
1985	Dr. Charles Lawrence
1988	The Very Rev. David Collins
1991	The Very Rev. David Collins
1994	Dr. Pamela Chinnis
1997	Dr. Pamela Chinnis
2000	Dr. Pamela Chinnis
2003	The Very Rev. George Werner
2006	The Very Rev. George Werner
2009	Dr. Bonnie Anderson
2012	Dr. Bonnie Anderson

Presiding Bishops since 1952

(with diocese from which resigned to take office as PB)

1947–1958	Bishop (Massachusetts) Henry Knox Sherrill
1958–1964	Bishop (Missouri) Arthur Lichtenberger
1964–1974	Bishop (Texas) John Elbridge Hines

1974–1985	Bishop (Mississippi) John Maury Allen
1986–1987	Bishop (Hawaii) Edmond Lee Browning
1998–2006	Bishop (Chicago) Frank Tracy Griswold III
2006–	Bishop (Nevada) Katharine Jefferts Schori

A note on the Authority of General Convention Resolutions

The President of the House of Deputies' Chancellor, Sally Johnson (a contributor to this collection of essays), has reflected on the question of the authority of General Convention resolutions (apart from those amending the Constitution and Canons) as follows:

There are many ways in which Resolutions of General Convention can be described. Some

- Take specific actions at a particular point in time, such as passing a budget to cover the triennium and set the assessment rate for diocesan support of the General Convention budget

- Direct dioceses, congregations, provinces and/or members of the church to do particular things

- Encourage dioceses, congregations, provinces and/or members to do certain things

- Encourage governmental and non-church entities to do certain things or take certain actions

- State the church's position on social issues

In its Opinion deciding whether or not a violation of a General Convention Resolution could be the basis for disciplinary action against a clergyperson under the Canons, the Court for the Trial of a Bishop declared:

General Convention has authority to pass Canons which are binding, and could, perhaps, adopt resolutions which clearly declare themselves to be mandatory, and which call for specific penalties when they are disobeyed.

Committees, Commissions, Agencies and Boards

Vanessa Glass

During the triennium between sessions, the General Convention continues its work—which is the work of the church—through Committees, Commissions, Agencies and Boards, also known as CCABs. CCABs fall into a variety of categories and are established either by resolution, canon, rules of order, or bylaws. When a CCAB is established, its mandate provides a directive for its work as well as defining the composition of its membership. Some of these bodies are geared primarily to preparing legislation or proposals for the next session of General Convention, including, for example, changes to the Constitution and Canons, or to the authorized liturgy of the church. Others are focused on developing programs and resources for mission and ministry. All of them are responsible to the church as a whole, acting in and through General Convention.

Before the National Council was established in 1919, CCABs were the primary means by which the work of the church was carried out. In 1916, there were 79 committees of the General Convention compared to the 25 Commissions and Committees in 2009.

Standing Commissions of the General Convention begin their work at the start of the triennium after the presiding officers appoint their members. A Convener is named to organize the first meeting and conduct an election of Chair, Vice Chair and Secretary. (GCO Handbook, I) Each officer has specific duties as outlined in the *Handbook for Committees, Commissions, Agencies, and Boards.*

CCABs may receive resolutions referred to them by the General Convention, generate policy recommendations, study areas of concern, or create resolutions. Resolutions created by CCABs are referred to as "A" resolutions when they are brought to the next session of Convention as part of their report.

In 2009, 419 pieces of legislation were received by the 76th General Convention of which 192 came from CCABs. (GCO Summary) In other words, close to half of the resolutions presented to the General Convention that year were generated by a Committee, Commission, Agency or Board.

The CCAB structure allows for additional time and concentrated study of important issues respecting the internal life and program of the church, and to weigh the mission concerns of the church in the world. At the end of the triennium CCABs report back to Convention through the official *Report to the ___ General Convention Otherwise Known as The Blue Book*, a triennial publication of the General Convention Office.

Committees, Commissions, Agencies and Boards date back to the earliest Conventions. They were created at each convention for a specific task. Most expired at the end of the triennium but some remained active as their ongoing work was deemed necessary. For example the [then] Standing Liturgical Commission, worked over several decades on the studies and proposals that would go to form the 1979 Book of Common Prayer. It successor, the Standing Commission on Liturgy and Music, has been charged with continued enrichment of the liturgical life of the church.

However, the House of Deputies Committee on the State of the Church holds the honor of being the oldest committee of the General Convention. It dates from 1792, and through the years it has played a major role in the structure and work of the Convention. In recent years this committee has synthesized and interpreted data and made recommendations to the General Convention through its *Blue Book* report and resolutions.

Executive Council

Established in 1919 (as the Board of Directors of the Domestic and Foreign Missionary Society), the National Council (now called the Executive Council) is canonically charged with unique powers and responsibilities on behalf of the General Convention. The Executive Council carries out the program and policies adopted by the General Convention. They are responsible for the coordination, development, and implementation of the ministry and mission of the church. Members sit for staggered terms of six years and are elected by the General Convention (20 members) and by the provinces (18 members). The Presiding Bishop is the *ex officio* Chair, and the President of the House of Deputies is the *ex officio* Vice Chair. The Secretary and the Treasurer of the Executive Council serve as non-voting members. (GCO Handbook, 1)

Standing Commissions

Standing Commissions are established in the canons and make recommendations on matters of continuing concern to the church. Each Standing Commission has a specific area of responsibility and is comprised of three bishops, three priests or deacons, and six lay persons. The Presiding Bishop appoints the bishops, and the President of the House of Deputies appoints all others. Members serve staggered six-year terms and do not have to be deputies. (GCO Handbook, 1)

Standing Commissions are the modern incarnation of areas of mission and ministry in which the church has long been involved. Membership size of the Standing Commissions varied from one to another until 2006, when it was standardized to consist of the twelve members described in the preceding paragraph. The mandate of Standing Commissions is generally to study and draft policy proposals on major subjects considered to be of continuing concern to the mission, worship, and program of the church.

Joint Standing Committees

Joint Standing Committees find their mandate in the Joint Rules of the Houses of General Convention and consider matters related to the work and function of the General Convention itself, rather than the overall life of the church. Members are appointed for three-years terms, and in some cases must be deputies or bishops, as is the case for serving on the Joint Standing Committee for Program, Budget and Finance. (GCO Handbook, 2)

Standing Committees of Executive Council

Standing Committees of Executive Council are written into the bylaws of the Executive Council. They study, review, and report on items that appear before the Council. Only Council members may serve.

Committees of Executive Council

Committees of Executive Council may be established by a General Convention resolution or by action of Executive Council. Committees created by either body have specific mandates to report through the Executive Council. For some committees created by General Convention, the duration of the committee expires at the end of the triennium. (GCO Handbook, 2) For committees created by Executive Council, their duration expires at the second General Convention following creation unless otherwise specified by the Council.

Ad Hoc Committees of Executive Council (Task Forces)

Ad hoc Committees are created by the Council to accomplish specific tasks, such as a feasibility study or research project, or to address a specific issue or concern. Ad hoc Committees are given a specific mandate and time frame for completing their work. The Council resolution that creates an ad hoc Committee must specify its composition; some members may be from outside of the Executive Council. (GCO Handbook, 2)

Task Forces of the General Convention

Task Forces are established by resolution of General Convention under Joint Rules of Order (IX.22). Their membership and mandate is defined at the time of creation. The resolution that creates the Task Force also includes an expiration date for the Task Force.

Committees of the House of Deputies or the House of Bishops

The presiding officer of each House has the authority under the Rules of Order of her House to appoint Committees with specific or ongoing responsibilities on behalf of the whole House. In 2009 at the close of the 76th General Convention, President of the House of Deputies Bonnie Anderson appointed the House of Deputies Special Study Committee on Church Governance and Polity "to present to the House of Deputies at the 77th General Convention, a study of the history, theology, political structure and practical realities of our church's governance and polity; and to make recommendations based on its findings to strengthen our self-understanding."

Likewise, the Presiding Bishop as the presiding officer of the House of Bishops has historically exercised this authority. The House of Bishops Committee on Theology was established by a 1964 House resolution, "to engage in continuing dialogue with contemporary theologians and report from time to time in order that this House may be better informed as to the nature of the crisis in the relationship between the language of Theology and that of modern culture."

Boards

Boards oversee semi-autonomous components of the church and can operate in one of three ways. They can be semi-autonomous (Board for Transition Ministries, Board of Archives); fully autonomous (Episcopal Relief & Development); or fully autonomous and independent (General Theological Seminary, the Church Pension Fund).

Agencies

Agencies are legally independent corporations affiliated with The Episcopal Church. Their affiliation lies in their own charters and by-laws. In general, their officers and boards are elected independently of the General Convention. Agencies have no canonical, legal or other reporting accountability to the General Convention or the Executive Council, however, they may have historic relationships to the church and may report their activities in the *Blue Book* and author

resolutions. Episcopal Relief and Development is an independent 501(c)
(3) corporation.

A List of CCABs

Following is a list of current Committees, Commissions, Agencies
and Boards from the 76th General Convention.[26]

Joint Standing Committees

Joint Standing Committee on Nominations
Joint Standing Committee on Planning and Arrangements
Joint Standing Committee on Program, Budget and Finance
Joint Committee for the Election of the Presiding Bishop

Committees of the House of Bishops

House of Bishops Committee on Pastoral Development
House of Bishops Planning Committee
House of Bishops Committee on Religious Communities
House of Bishops Theology Committee
House Bishops Spouses' Planning Group

Committees of the House of Deputies

House of Deputies Committee on the State of the Church
Task Group on the Rules of Order of the House of Deputies

Standing Commissions Created by the General Convention

Anglican and International Peace with Justice Concerns
Communication and Information Technology
Constitution and Canons
Mission and Evangelism of The Episcopal Church
Ecumenical and Interreligious Relations
Health
Lifelong Christian Formation and Education
Liturgy and Music
Ministry Development
Social Justice and Public Policy

---

[26] For a critique and a call for reform of the CCAB structure see, "Standing Commissions in the Twenty-First Century: A
Case for Reform" by the Rev. Alexander H. ("Sandy") Webb II, in the *Journal of Episcopal Church Canon Law.*

Small Congregations
Stewardship and Development
Structure of the Church
World Mission

Committees and Task Forces Created by the General Convention

Joint Audit Committee of the Executive Council and the DFMS
Executive Council Committee on Anti-Racism
Executive Council Committee on HIV/AIDS
Executive Council Committee on Science, Technology and Faith
Executive Council Committee on the Status of Women
Budgetary Funding Task Force
Title IV Task Force II – Education
Title IV Review Committee
Historiographer of The Episcopal Church

Committees Created by the Executive Council

Joint Investment Committee
Episcopal News Service Advisory Committee
Episcopal Archives Strategy Committee
Executive Council Committee on Corporate Social Responsibility
Executive Council Committee on Indigenous Ministries
Economic Justice Loan Committee

Agencies and Boards

Board of the Archives of The Episcopal Church
Board for Transition Ministry
The Church Pension Fund
Episcopal Church Building Fund
Episcopal Relief and Development
General Board of Examining Chaplains
Forward Movement Publications

How to Participate:
A Word to Deputies

Katherine Tyler Scott

The oft-repeated adage, "Knowledge is power," is very applicable when examining the roles and responsibilities of deputies in The Episcopal Church. Knowledge is also identity, and this collection of essays can be a beginning resource for obtaining relevant information and the necessary education for those wanting to participate.

Leadership in The Episcopal Church involves an obligation to continue to learn about the history, mission, polity, and governance of The Episcopal Church. Lay leaders as well as priests and deacons are charged to study such matters and remain current with the state of things. Having such knowledge enables lay and clergy leaders to claim the authority bestowed upon them in the Baptismal Covenant in which all share.

While there are numerous opportunities to serve and participate in the General Convention as a deputy, such service and participation entail special responsibilities.

Be Prepared

Being a deputy to General Convention comes with a duty to be well prepared. Numerous resources have been provided in recent years to assist in that preparation. This can include your subscribing to the House of Bishops and Deputies ListServe (HoB/D), and taking part in the President of the House of Deputies on-line discussion forum,[27] Deputies are also charged with completing the form indicating preferences for a legislative committee assignment, reading (and responding when requested to) the communiqués sent throughout the triennium by the President of the House of Deputies, attending all meetings of your deputation, and reading all of the *Blue Book* reports and resolutions when published in preparation for the General Convention.

In practice, first-time deputies are not normally assigned to a legislative committee. This gives them valuable time to observe, listen, and learn without excessive pressure to perform effectively and manage complexity skillfully. Deputies who are not assigned are free to attend legislative committee meetings and hearings, and are encouraged to do so. Some deputations assign deputies who are not appointed to a committee by the President to attend the hearings and meetings of one or more specific committees. Such a deputy is asked to report to the deputation and help everyone to be well-informed about a variety of issues coming before the General Convention. Deputies unassigned to a committee who have been deputies before can participate in this manner also. This is very helpful to the colleagues who *are* assigned to committees, as their committee work necessitates close focus on the issues coming before the committee on which they serve, and they do not have ample opportunity to attend the hearings or sessions of other committees.

Fulfill Committee Responsibilities

Deputies who receive notification of a committee assignment will hear from the appointed Chair of the Committee about the organization, structure, schedule, membership and process of the work during General Convention. Read what is sent and don't hesitate to ask questions so there is clarity about expectations. It is also suggested that in addition to reading all of the legislation assigned to the committee, go online to the Archives and review resolutions assigned to the Committee at previous General Conventions. The Archives are a wonderful resource for becoming better informed.

If appointed to a committee, deputies are obligated to attend *all* of

---

[27] Both of these electronic resources require a willingness to engage with the latest technology, and have proven invaluable in sharing information and framing discussions of issues prior to the General Convention meetings.

the committee's meetings and hearings, and to keep track of the status of resolutions in the legislative process. Be prepared to speak on the floor, and be ready to clarify, explain and/or support or oppose the resolution being considered by the House.

Obviously, deputies must honor the rules and decorum of the House. If you speak on the floor, adhere to the rules; do not repeat what other deputies have already said. If deputies have any questions about procedure, protocol, or process they should not hesitate to ask a senior deputy—someone who has attended at least seven General Conventions—for assistance. Senior Deputies are designated as such on their name-tags, and their deputation standard displaying the name of the diocese will have a yellow ribbon attached to it.

It is highly recommended that all deputies participate in the worship services and in discussion groups with others attending the General Convention as they are scheduled.

Communicate the Actions of the GC

Once General Convention ends, a new phase of responsibility begins for deputies. Within a reasonable time the chair of each deputation will schedule a meeting of the deputies to debrief the General Convention experience and actions. A report may need to be prepared for submission to their bishop, the Standing Committee, the Diocesan Convention, and to their respective parishes. When the General Convention Office sends the report of General Convention Actions and Resolutions the deputation needs to meet and review it. They will need to heed those resolutions pertaining to dioceses and determine which ones (and in what form) are to be presented to the Diocesan Convention for information, deliberation or action. A report of the diocesan action on these resolutions is to be sent to the General Convention Office. The deputy remains a deputy until an election is held and another is elected—the obligation to educate parishes and dioceses is not negotiable; it is a key responsibility of deputies.

Meetings about the General Convention's actions should be scheduled immediately after the General Convention. Deputies should make sure that their report on Convention actions is widely distributed, for example, through the diocesan website, newsletter, and meetings.

One Step Beyond:
The Wider Church

Tobias Stanislas Haller BSG

In addition to its internal governance and polity, The Episcopal Church enjoys a number of relationships with other ecclesiastical bodies. While it is beyond the scope of this study to enter into a detailed discussion of these relationships, note should be taken that they are reflected in our governing documents, and in the day-to-day work of the church. These relationships fall roughly into two categories: the historical relationships of the members of the Anglican Communion, and the relationships of full communion into which The Episcopal Church has entered over the years. In both cases the General Convention makes the final determination concerning The Episcopal Church's role in the relationships.

The Anglican Communion

The Episcopal Church inherits much of its identity from the Church of England. From the outset, this kinship and inheritance was recognized as a historical fact. Beyond having derived at least one strand of episcopal succession from the Church of England (the other strand being from the disestablished Scottish Episcopal Church's bishops through Seabury), there was scant interaction between The Episcopal Church, once given constitutional foundation, and the "Mother Church" for the first several decades of the newly independent church's life.[28] While the

---

[28] See Bishop Paul Marshall's "Note on the Role of North America in the Evolution of Anglicanism" in the Fall 2005 *Anglican Theological Review* (87:4, 549-557) for a detailed analysis of this interaction, or lack thereof.

Archbishops of Canterbury and York referred to the "spiritual commu-nion" that existed between the two churches[29], when American writers used the term "communion" from the time of foundation up until the mid-nineteenth century, they were almost invariably referring to the *internal* fellowship of the church in the various states (later dioceses). This usage continued even when the Anglican Communion began to have a sense of conscious identity with the calling of the first Lambeth Conference in 1867.

It was a hundred years later (in the two Conventions of 1964 and 1967 required for Constitutional amendment) that formal recognition of the Anglican Communion, and The Episcopal Church's participa-tion in it, made its way into a Preamble added to the Constitution. This Preamble states that The Episcopal Church is

> ...a constituent member of the Anglican Communion, a Fellowship within the One, Holy, Catholic, and Apostolic Church, of those duly constituted Dioceses, Provinces, and regional Churches in communion with the See of Canterbury, upholding and propagating the historic Faith and Order as set forth in the Book of Common Prayer.

There has been some discussion in recent years as to whether this language is descriptive or prescriptive; that is, does it describe a histor-ical reality or establish a requirement that The Episcopal Church always be a part of the Anglican Communion as defined, "in communion with the See of Canterbury"? From the English side, the Canons of the Church of England (note on Canon C8, and Rule 54(5) of the Church Representation Rules) assign the authority to determine, should any doubt arise, with whom the Church of England is in communion jointly to the Archbishops of Canterbury and York.

Apart from the Preamble, communion status becomes a matter of some practicality when the recognition and/or licensing of clergy is concerned, and the mutual recognition and interchangeability of clergy

---

[29] "Letter to the Committee of General Convention, 1786," in White's *Memoirs*, note 9. It is also noteworthy that whatever the nature of "spiritual communion" enjoyed, the Act of Parliament that permitted the Archbishops to confer the episcopate on White and Provoost specified "that no person or persons consecrated to the office of a bishop in the manner aforesaid, nor any person or persons deriving their consecration from or under any bishops so consecrated, nor any person or persons admitted to the order of deacon or priest by any bishop or bishops so consecrated, or by the successor or successors of any bishop or bishops so consecrated, shall be thereby enabled to exercise his or their respective office or offices within his Majesty's dominions." (ibid., note 10.)

often becomes the defining "limit" to ecumenical and other relationships. Both The Episcopal Church (Canon III.10) and the Church of England (Section 6[2] of the Overseas and Other Clergy [Ministry and Ordination] Measure 1967) make further reference to churches "in communion." A comparison of the rules of the Church of England (in the note to C8 referenced above) and The Episcopal Church (at Canon I.20) indicates that there are churches with which either The Episcopal Church or the Church of England is in communion that are not in communion with the other. (See the following note on churches outside the Anglican Communion.)

Clergy to one side, however, there is additional reference to "communion with the See of Canterbury" in the Canon (III.14) governing religious orders and other Christian communities, which raises the same question concerning the nature of "communion" and whether it is with the Archbishop of Canterbury, the See of Canterbury, or the Church of England, and whether such communion is personal or corporate. (The language in this canon is ambiguous, as it refers to "a society of Christians in communion with the See of Canterbury..."— it appears that the *society* as a whole rather than the individual members is intended—but this raises the question as to who determines who is "in communion" with whom.[30])

The Anglican Communion itself, until the mid–nineteenth century, was a fairly loosely formed and self-described "fellowship" that emerged from the historical realities of English (and by then to a significant extent American) colonial and missionary efforts. By that time, the Communion had begun to evolve some mechanisms or "instruments" to facilitate the relationships and common mission work of the members of the Communion. A short overview of these "instruments of communion" appears in the *Windsor Report* (paragraphs 97ff., noting they are there referred to as "instruments of *unity*"—a term revised in subsequent discussion). Briefly, the four consist of the Archbishop of Canterbury as "first among equals," the Lambeth Conference of

---

[30] The canons of TEC also lack a clear definition of **communion**, apart from what can be inferred from the listing of churches with which TEC is in full communion forming the bulk of Canon I.20. The published edition of the Canons of the Church of England includes a similar list (on page 208 of the sixth edition), with an appended opinion that in doubtful cases, as noted above, it is up to the Archbishops of Canterbury and York acting jointly to rule on whether a church is in communion with the Church of England or not. There is no reference to communion with individuals or societies of Christians.

Bishops (first assembled in 1867 and still convened by the Archbishop), the Anglican Consultative Council (a representative body including lay, clerical and episcopal members from all of the Communion members, established in its final form in 1968), and the Primates' Meeting, a gathering of the chief bishop of each church or province (by whatever title identified) which began meeting in 1978. Of these "instruments" only the Anglican Consultative Council has a formal constitution. The Canons of The Episcopal Church (I.4.2.g) assign the task of electing its representatives to the ACC to the Executive Council.

Efforts at the level of the Communion to develop (or not) some additional pan-Anglican governing structures—or to give greater authority to those that already exist short of governance—is part of an ongoing conversation in which The Episcopal Church plays a significant and committed role. The Proposed Anglican Covenant is a part of that ongoing process. In the meantime, there is considerable exploration of the nature of autonomy (self-governance) and the degree to which any church or province of the Communion may choose to limit its own autonomy.

Christian Fellowship and Communion

The latter quarter of the twentieth century also brought a number of ecumenical dialogues to fruition in the establishment of The Episcopal Church's full communion with the Evangelical Lutheran Church in America and the Northern and Southern Provinces of the Moravian Church in America, joining the churches with which communion had already been established by that time (the Old Catholic Churches of the Union of Utrecht, the Philippine Independent Church and the Mar Thoma Syrian Church of Malabar). These communion relationships were established by means of covenants and concordats that laid out the terms of communion, in particular regarding the degree and manner in which ministry could be shared or interchangeable. The communion relationships are specified in Canon I.20.

Among the constitutional limits The Episcopal Church has established for itself is the respect shown to the geographical integrity of churches with which we are in communion, in permitting the creation of missionary dioceses only in areas not already part of a church-in-communion. (CC Article VI.1) As noted above, various constitutional and canonical regulations govern the roles and functions of clergy from other churches. (Note especially the constitutional requirements in Article VIII.)

While most of the canonical concern in these relationships revolves around clergy, these communion relationships provide all of the churches' members the opportunity to learn from one another and to cooperate in the work of mission and ministry.

Some Closing Reflections

Ernie Bennett

The purpose of this publication is to present a study of the history, theology, political structure and practical realities of our church's governance and polity, and

- to explain why we believe it is essential to empower each order of ministry "to take their place in the governance of the Church" and

- to consider
  » what kind of theology is embodied in such a polity;
  » what strengths flow from our system of government, and
  » what challenges this presents; and

- to make recommendations based on its findings to strengthen our self-understanding.

We believe that the use of this resource, and others that may be developed, is a particular way of accomplishing the last of these points.

There seems little argument from a historical point of view that two separate Houses have been an integral part of our governance structure from the beginning. The only real debate in terms of the necessity for both Houses historically seems to have been in the area of determining what sort of vote was needed to override the will of the other body. S.D. McConnell, in his *History of the American Episcopal Church* published in 1916, observes that in the Constitution of 1789 "clergy and laity could pass any measure over [the House of Bishops'] heads by a four-fifths vote, or through the Bishops' failure to negative it within a limited period of two days. Twenty years later both these restrictions upon independent action were removed, and the House of Bishops received the power which has often stood the Church in good stead." (II.5)

In *Many Parts, One Body,* James Dator with Jan Nunley observe that: "Until the constitutional revision of 1901, it was still necessary that the Bishops give their 'approbation or disapprobation' in writing, in either case within three days, or an act by the Deputies would become law without the Bishops' concurrence." (58) One need not search very far for historical evidence that the governance of The Episcopal Church was constituted from the start by laity and clergy, supplemented by bishops when the latter were first ordained for, and then by, The Episcopal Church.

In the Catechism (BCP, 855-6) we are taught that the "Church carries out its mission through the ministry of all its members" and that "The ministers of the Church are lay persons, bishops, priests, and deacons." The laity are to "represent Christ and his Church; to bear witness to him wherever they may be; and, according to the gifts given them, to carry on Christ's work of reconciliation in the world; and to take their place in the life, worship, and governance of the Church." Priests are to "represent Christ and his Church, particularly as pastor to the people; to share with the bishop in the overseeing of the Church,"[31] while deacons are to "represent Christ and his Church, particularly as a servant of those in need; and to assist bishops and priests in the proclamation of the Gospel and the administration of the sacraments." We are incomplete without the ministry of one another.

In his Arrington Lectures, 1982, at the University of the South, the Rev. Canon James R. Gundrum, D.D., then Executive Officer of the General Convention, quotes from F.V. Mills in his book *Bishops by Ballot*: "The scepter was separated from the mitre."

> From 1789 forward, bishops and budgets were both brought forward by ballot in all places including the General Convention by clergy and laity, meeting together and voting together. This simple phenomenon was unique, and indeed revolutionary—as revolutionary as the American Revolution itself.

---

[31] At the examination in ordination (BCP, 531) it is put this way: "…to take your share in the councils of the Church."

The actions of the churchmen between 1782 and 1789 marked a stunning reversal of ecclesiastical tradition, one which has, for whatever reasons, remained long-hidden from view and from the understanding of those who attend the General Convention, and from the Church in general. Without question, it was the direct intention of [The Episcopal Church] ...to eliminate any use of the medieval concept of a magisterial prince-bishop, appointed by and responsible to the king, which was the case in England from the time of William I. Rather, The Episcopal Church quite consciously re-captured the primitive episcopate wholly separate from the state. They determined also that bishops were to be servants of the Church and not its lords.

He then goes on to quote a church historian (and a professor of mine):

As John Woolverton, in his review of Mills' book, so aptly stated it, "Today in The Episcopal Church in particular... there is a tendency to ignore the late eighteenth century lesson of American ecclesiastical democracy. This tendency is manifested, for example,...in the action of the House of Bishops taken apart from the laity and clergy of General Convention in announcing a 'conscience clause' for those clerics opposed to the legally approved ordination of women. Moreover, the increasing authority of the Lambeth Conference of Anglican Bishops, the move to have Anglican prelates meet bi-annually, apart from the clergy and laity of the Anglican Consultative Council—and the casual talk at Lambeth, 1978, of freeing the Archbishop of Canterbury from both his diocesan and national responsibilities in England and become a sort of Anglican pope, all serve to show how little the lessons of the 1780s have been learned."

Ours is a messy method of governance but it is worth contending for. As the late Dr. Pamela Chinnis, speaking at St. Phillip's, Laurel, Maryland in the fall of 1991, put it succinctly,

More and more we see efforts to increase the role and power of the House of Bishops and the national church staff. We have every right to be concerned. Eternal vigilance is the price of freedom from a church dominated by the House of Bishops.

Perhaps a little overstated, but it reveals the passion and zeal for our church from a dearly beloved servant and leader of our church. To lose sight of the genius and rich heritage of our form of governance would be to follow Esau in his trade of a rich blessing for a bowl of red pottage. (Genesis 25:29–34)

Bibliography

References and suggestions for further reading

Note: Some of the older source documents appear in multiple editions, and many are now available in electronic format from one or more on-line sites, such as Google Books.

Archives of the Episcopal Church. 1999. *Provinces and the General Convention.*

————."A History of Executive Council."

————.2010. "Research Report: Committees, Commissions, Boards and Agencies." December 17, 2010

————.2011. "Research Report: House of Bishops Interim Meetings." June 14, 2011.

Armentrout, Don S. and Robert Boak Slocum. 1994. *Documents of Witness: a history of the Episcopal Church, 1782-1985.* New York: Church Hymnal Corporation.

Barnds, William Joseph. 1958. "A Study of the Development of the Office of Presiding Bishop of the American Episcopal Church 1794-1944." *Historical Magazine of the Episcopal Church.* XXVI (December, 1958), 254-86.

Barnes, C. Rankin. 1951. *The General Convention Offices and Officers 1785-1950.* New York: Church Historical Society.

Bayne Jr., Stephen. 1963. *Mutual Responsibility and Independence in the Body of Christ,* New York: Seabury Press.

BB. The "Blue Book" of General Convention (reports submitted by Committees, Commissions, Agencies and Boards in advance of Conventions). Noted by year of Convention.

BCP. Book of Common Prayer (page references are to the 1979 edition. Other versions are noted by their date of authorization.)

Booz, Allen & Hamilton. 1971. *National Organization Study of the Protestant Episcopal Church in the United States of America.* (A report submitted to the 1973 Convention).

Borg, Marcus and John Dominic Crossan. 2009. *The First Paul.* San Francisco: Harper Collins.

Burtchaell, James Tunstead. 1992. *From Synagogue to Church: Public Services and Offices in the Earliest Christian Communities*. Cambridge: Cambridge University Press.

CC. *Constitution and Canons for the Government of the Protestant Episcopal Church in the United States of America &c*. (Citations are to the 2009 version. Other versions are noted by date.)

Chinnis, Pamela. 2000.*Decently and in Order*. Ed. Pamela Darling. Cincinnati, Ohio: Forward Movement Publications.

Collins, David. 1996. *There is a Lad Here. A Book of Gratitude*. Darien, Ga.: Darien News.

Colliver, Albert. "The Origin of the Term *Laity*."

Dator, James. 2011. "Where Is The Locus Of Authority Within The Episcopal Church?" *Journal of Episcopal Church Canon Law*. Vol 2, No 1, February 2011, 131–190.

Dator, James and Jan Nunley. 2010. *Many Parts, One Body: How the Episcopal Church Works*. New York: Church Publishing Inc.

Douglas, Ian. 1996. *Fling Out the Banner: The National Church Ideal and the Foreign Mission of the Episcopal Church*. New York: The Church Hymnal Corporation.

Dozier, Verna. 1988. *The Calling of the Laity: Verna Dozier Anthology*. Washington, D.C.: Alban Institute.

Dozier, Verna J. with Celia Hahn, 1982. *The Authority of the Laity*. Washington, D.C.: The Alban Institute.

Ehrman, Bart. 2005. *After the New Testament: The Writings of the Apostolic Fathers*. Chantilly, Virginia: The Teaching Company. (A recorded lecture series.)

Evenbeck, Scott and Katherine Tyler Scott. 2000, 2003. "An Orientation to General Convention" for Province V.

Executive Council and the Domestic and Foreign Missionary Society, 1923-2009. By-Laws.

Executive Council. Reports from Meetings, available at the Archives of the Episcopal Church and at Episcopalchurch.org

Foster, Roland. 1982. *The Role of the Presiding Bishop*. Cincinnati: Forward Movement.

GCO Handbook. General Convention Office. Handbook for Committees, Commissions, Agencies and Boards 2010 – 2012.

GCO Summary. General Convention Office. Summary of Actions of the 76th General Convention. 2009.

Griffiss, James. 1997. *The Anglican Vision*. Cambridge, Mass.: Cowley Publications.

Guilbert, Charles M. 1981. "Changes in the Structure, Organization, and Government of the Episcopal Church in the Last Sixty Years." Unpublished manuscript, available through the Episcopal Church Archives.

Holmes, David L. 1993. *A Brief History of the Episcopal Church*. Harrisburg, Pa.: Trinity Press International.

Hooker, Richard. *Of the Lawes of Ecclesiastical Politie*. (Numerous editions are available, and citations are by book and section.)

House of Bishops. 2009. "Bishops' Statement on the Polity of the Episcopal Church."

JGC. 1967. "Report of the Mutual Responsibility Commission."

JGC. 1976. "Report of the Standing Commission on the Structure of the Church."

JGC. Journal of the General Convention. (Indicated by year of the Convention.)

Johnson, Sally. 2007. *Analysis of Authority in the Episcopal Church.*

Loveland, Clara. 1956. *The Critical Years: the reconstitution of the Anglican Church in the United States of America: 1780-1789.* New York: Seabury Press.

Marshall, Paul V. 2005. "A Note on the Role of North America in the Evolution of Anglicanism" in the *Anglican Theological Review* Vol 87, No 4, Fall 2005. 549-557.

McConnell, S. D. *History of the American Episcopal Church 1600-1915.* 1916. (Available online at Project Canterbury.)

Mills, Fred V. 1978. *Bishops by Ballot: an eighteenth century ecclesiastical revolution.* Oxford University Press.

Perry, William Stevens. 1881. *A Handbook of the General Convention of The Protestant Episcopal Church, giving its History and Constitution.* Thomas Whittaker. (Republished by Bibliofile without date)

Prichard, Robert W. 1999. *A History of the Episcopal Church.* Harrisburg, Pa.: Morehouse Publishing.

Royce, Robert C. 2009. "The Roles, Duties and Responsibilities of the Executive Council, Domestic and Foreign Missionary Society, Presiding Bishop and President of the House of Deputies in the Governance of the Episcopal Church." Monograph available through Episcopal Church Archives.

Stevick, Daniel B. 1965. *Canon Law: A Handbook.* New York: Seabury Press. (A second edition was published by HarperCollins 1983).

Stone, John S. 1844. *Memoir of the Life of The Rt. Rev. Alexander Viets Griswold.* Philadelphia: Stavely and McCalla. (Republished by Cornell University Digital Library without date).

Stringfellow, William. 1994. *A Keeper of the Word: Selected Writings of William Stringfellow,* ed. Bill Wylie Kellerman. Grand Rapids, Mich.: Eerdmans.

Syndor, William. 1980. *Looking at the Episcopal Church.* Harrisburg, Pa.: Morehouse Publishing.

Taylor, Frederick William. 1898. "The Provincial System," in *The Church Standard* July 23, 1898

Thompsett, Fredrica Harris. 1989. *We Are Theologians.* Cambridge, Mass.: Cowley Press.

————.2010."Coming to Our Sacramental Senses: Full Baptismal Participation and Full Inclusion of the People of God," in *God's Call and Our Response.* Chicago, Ill.: Chicago Consultation.

Tiffany, Charles Comfort. 1895.*A History of the Protestant Episcopal Church in the United States.* New York: The Christian Literature Company. (Volume VII of the American Church History Series.)

TPS. Trinity Church New York. 1870. "The Provincial System."

Wallace, Bob, N. 1976. *The General Convention of the Episcopal Church*. New York: Seabury Press.

Wand, J. W. C. *The Anglican Communion: A Survey*. Oxford University Press, 1948.

W.D. White, Edwin Augustine, and Jackson A. Dykman. 1981. *Annotated Constitution and Canons for the Government of the Episcopal Church,* New York: Seabury Press. (This is a revision of the 1954 edition, to which reference is also made with that year noted.)

Webb II, Alexander H. 2009. "On Canon Law (Canon 1.1.2)." Virginia Theological Seminary. (Unpublished paper.)

———. 2010. "Standing Commissions in the Twenty-First Century: A Case for Reform." *Journal of Episcopal Church Canon Law.* Vol 1, Number 1, July 2010, 23-32.

White, Edwin Augustine. 1924. *Constitution and Canons for the Government of the Protestant Episcopal Church in the United States of America*. New York: Edwin S. Gorham.

White, William. 1782. *The Case of the Episcopal Churches in the United States Considered.* (Various editions available, one being extracted from William Stevens Perry's *Journals of General Conventions of the Protestant Episcopal Church.* Claremont, N.H.: The Claremont Manufacturing Company, 1874, pp. 420–36. A more recent edition is that of Richard Salomon, Church Historical Society, 1954.)

———.1820. *Memoirs of the Protestant Episcopal Church: from its organization up to the present day*. Philadelphia: S. Potter & Co.

Windsor Report, The. 2004. From the Lambeth Commission on Communion, and available at http://anglicancommunion.org/windsor2004/